I. INTRODUCTION

The Sex Offender Registration and Notification Act ("SORNA" or "the Act"), which is title I of the Adam Walsh Child Protection and Safety Act of 2006 (P.L. 109-248), provides a new comprehensive set of minimum standards for sex offender registration and notification in the United States. These Guidelines are issued to provide guidance and assistance to covered jurisdictions—the 50 States, the District of Columbia, the principal U.S. territories, and Indian tribal governments—in implementing the SORNA standards in their registration and notification programs.

The adoption of these Guidelines carries out a statutory directive to the Attorney General, appearing in SORNA § 112(b), to issue guidelines to interpret and implement SORNA. Other provisions of SORNA establish the Office of Sex Offender Sentencing, Monitoring, Apprehending, Registering, and Tracking (the "SMART Office"), a component of the Office of Justice Programs of the U.S. Department of Justice. The SMART Office is authorized by law to administer the standards for sex offender registration and notification that are set forth in SORNA and interpreted and implemented in these Guidelines. It is further authorized to cooperate with and provide assistance to states, local governments, tribal governments, and other public and private entities in relation to sex offender registration and notification and other measures for the protection of the public from sexual abuse or exploitation. *See* SORNA § 146(c). Accordingly, the SMART Office should be regarded by jurisdictions discharging registration and notification functions as their key partner and resource in the federal government in further developing and strengthening their sex offender registration and notification programs, and the SMART Office will provide all possible assistance for this purpose.

The development of sex offender registration and notification programs in the United States has proceeded rapidly since the early 1990s, and at the present time such programs exist in all of the states, the District of Columbia, and some of the territories and tribes. These programs serve a number of important public safety purposes. In their most basic character, the registration aspects of these programs are systems for tracking sex offenders following their release into the community. If a sexually violent crime occurs or a child is molested, information available to law enforcement through the registration program about sex offenders who may have been present in the area may help to identify the perpetrator and solve the crime. If a particular released sex offender is implicated in such a crime, knowledge of the sex offender's whereabouts through the registration system may help law enforcement in making a prompt apprehension. The registration program may also have salutary effects in relation to the likelihood of registrants committing more sex offenses. Registered sex offenders will perceive that the authorities' knowledge of their identities, locations, and past offenses reduces the chances that they can avoid detection and apprehension if they reoffend, and this perception may help to discourage them from engaging in further criminal conduct.

Registration also provides the informational base for the other key aspect of the programs—notification—which involves making information about released sex offenders more broadly available to the public. The means of public notification currently include sex offender websites in all states, the District of Columbia, and some territories, and may involve other forms of notice as well. The availability of such information helps members of the public to take common sense measures for the protection of themselves and their families, such as declining the offer of a convicted child molester to watch their children or head a youth group, or reporting to the authorities approaches to children or other suspicious activities by such a sex offender. Here as well, the effect is salutary in relation to the sex offenders themselves, since knowledge by those around them of their sex offense histories reduces the likelihood that they will be presented with opportunities to reoffend.

While sex offender registration and notification in the United States are generally carried out through programs operated by the individual states and other non-federal jurisdictions, their effectiveness depends on also having effective arrangements for tracking of registrants as they move among jurisdictions and some national baseline of registration and notification standards. In a federal union like the United States with a mobile population, sex offender registration could not be effective if registered sex offenders could simply disappear from the purview of the registration authorities by moving from one jurisdiction to another, or if registration and notification requirements could be evaded by moving from a jurisdiction with an effective program to a nearby jurisdiction that required little or nothing in terms of registration and notification.

Hence, there have been national standards for sex offender registration in the United States since the enactment of the Jacob Wetterling Crimes Against Children and Sexually Violent Offender Act (42 U.S.C. 14071) in 1994. The national standards from their inception have addressed such matters as the offenses for which registration should be required, updating and periodic verification of registration information, the duration of registration, public notification, and continued registration and tracking of sex offenders when they relocate from one jurisdiction to another.

Following the enactment of the Wetterling Act in 1994, that Act was amended a number of times, in part reflecting and in part promoting trends in the development of the state registration and notification programs. Ultimately, Congress concluded that the patchwork of standards that had resulted from piecemeal amendments should be replaced with a comprehensive new set of standards—the SORNA reforms, whose implementation these Guidelines concern—that would close potential gaps and loopholes under the old law, and generally strengthen the nationwide network of sex offender registration and notification programs. Important areas of reform under the SORNA standards include:

- Extending the jurisdictions in which registration is required beyond the 50 States, the District of Columbia, and the principal U.S. territories, to include Indian tribal jurisdictions.

- Extending the classes of sex offenders and sex offenses for which registration is required.

- Consistently requiring that sex offenders in the covered classes register and keep the registration current in the jurisdictions in which they reside, work, or go to school.

4

THE NATIONAL GUIDELINES FOR SEX OFFENDER REGISTRATION AND NOTIFICATION

CONTENTS

- Requiring more extensive registration information.

- Adding to the national standards periodic in-person appearances by registrants to verify and update the registration information.

- Broadening the availability of information concerning registered sex offenders to the public, through posting on sex offender websites and by other means.

- Adopting reforms affecting the required duration of registration.

In addition, SORNA strengthens the federal superstructure elements that leverage and support the sex offender registration and notification programs of the registration jurisdictions. These strengthened elements are: (i) stepped-up federal investigation and prosecution efforts to assist jurisdictions in enforcing sex offender registration requirements; (ii) new statutory provisions for the national database and national website (i.e., the National Sex Offender Registry and the Dru Sjodin National Sex Offender Public Website) that effectively compile information obtained under the registration programs of the states and other jurisdictions and make it readily available to law enforcement or the public on a nationwide basis; (iii) development by the federal government of software tools, which the states and other registration jurisdictions will be able to use to facilitate the operation of their registration and notification programs in conformity with the SORNA standards; and (iv) establishment of the SMART Office to administer the national standards for sex offender registration and notification and to assist registration jurisdictions in their implementation.

Through the cooperative effort of the 50 States, the District of Columbia, the U.S. territories, and Indian tribal governments with the responsible federal agencies, the SORNA goal of an effective and comprehensive national system of registration and notification programs can be realized, with great benefit to the ultimate objective of "protect[ing] the public from sex offenders and offenders against children." SORNA § 102. These Guidelines provide the blueprint for that effort.

II.   GENERAL PRINCIPLES

Before turning to the specific SORNA standards and requirements discussed in the remainder of these Guidelines, certain general points should be noted concerning the interpretation and application of the Act and these Guidelines:

A. Terminology

These Guidelines use key terms with the meanings defined in SORNA. In particular, the term "jurisdiction" is consistently used with the meaning set forth in SORNA § 111(10). As defined in that provision, it refers to the 50 States, the District of Columbia, the five principal U.S. territories—i.e., the Commonwealth of Puerto Rico, Guam, American Samoa, the Northern Mariana Islands, and the United States Virgin Islands—and Indian tribes that elect to function as registration jurisdictions under SORNA § 127. (For more concerning covered jurisdictions, *see*

Part III of these Guidelines.) Thus, when these Guidelines refer to "jurisdictions " implementing the SORNA registration and notification requirements, the reference is to implementation of these requirements by the jurisdictions specified in SORNA § 111(10). "Jurisdictions" is not used to refer to other territorial or political units or subdivisions, such as counties, cities, or towns of states or territories. Likewise, the term "sex offense" is not used to refer to any and all crimes of a sexual nature, but rather to those covered by the definition of "sex offense " appearing in SORNA § 111(5), and the term "sex offender" has the meaning stated in SORNA § 111(1). (For more concerning covered sex offenses and offenders, *see* Part IV of these Guidelines.)

SORNA's registration requirements generally come into play when sex offenders are released from imprisonment, or when they are sentenced if the sentence does not involve imprisonment. *See* SORNA § 113(b). "Imprisonment " as it is used in SORNA and these Guidelines refers to incarceration pursuant to a conviction, regardless of the nature of the institution in which the offender serves the sentence. It is not used in any narrow technical sense, such as confinement in a state "prison" as opposed to a local "jail."

SORNA includes a number of references relating to implementation by jurisdictions of the requirements of "this title." Section 125 provides a mandatory 10% reduction in certain federal justice assistance funding for jurisdictions that fail, as determined by the Attorney General, to substantially implement "this title" within the time frame specified in section 124, and section 126 authorizes a Sex Offender Management Assistance grant program to help offset the costs of implementing "this title." In the context of these provisions, the references to "this title" function as a shorthand for the SORNA sex offender registration and notification standards. They do not mean that funding under these provisions is affected by a jurisdiction's implementation or non-implementation of reforms unrelated to sex offender registration and notification that appear in later portions of title I of the Adam Walsh Child Protection and Safety Act of 2006 (particularly, subtitle C of that title).

Section 125(d) of SORNA states that the provisions of SORNA "that are cast as directions to jurisdictions or their officials constitute, in relation to States, only conditions required to avoid the reduction of Federal funding under this section." Statements in these Guidelines that SORNA requires jurisdictions to adopt certain measures should be understood accordingly in their application to the states. Since the SORNA requirements relating to sex offender registration and notification are, in relation to the states, only partial funding eligibility conditions, creation of these requirements is within the constitutional authority of the federal government.

B. Minimum National Standards

SORNA establishes a national baseline for sex offender registration and notification programs. In other words, the Act generally constitutes a set of *minimum* national standards and sets a floor, not a ceiling, for jurisdictions' programs. Hence, for example, a jurisdiction may have a system that requires registration by broader classes of convicted offenders than those identified in SORNA, or that requires, in addition, registration by certain classes of non-convicts (such as persons acquitted on the ground of insanity of sexually violent crimes or child molestation offenses, or persons released following civil commitment as sexually dangerous persons). A jurisdiction may require verification of the registered address or other registration information by sex offenders with greater frequency than SORNA requires, or by other means in addition to those required by SORNA (e.g., through the use of mailed address verification forms, in addition to in-person appearances). A jurisdiction may require sex offenders to register for longer periods than those required by the SORNA standards. A jurisdiction may require that changes in registration information be reported by registrants on a more stringent basis than the SORNA minimum standards—e.g., requiring that changes of residence be reported before the sex offender moves, rather than within three business days following the move. A jurisdiction may extend website posting to broader classes of registrants than SORNA requires and may post more information concerning registrants than SORNA and these Guidelines require.

Such measures, which encompass the SORNA baseline of sex offender registration and notification requirements but go beyond them, generally have no negative implication concerning jurisdictions' implementation of or compliance with SORNA. This is so because the general purpose of SORNA is to protect the public from sex offenders and offenders against children through effective sex offender registration and notification, and it is not intended to preclude or limit jurisdictions' discretion to adopt more extensive or additional registration and notification requirements to that end. There is an exception to this general rule in SORNA § 118(b), which requires that certain types of information, such as victim identity and registrants' Social Security numbers, be excluded from jurisdictions' publicly accessible sex offender websites, as discussed in Part VII of these Guidelines. In other respects, jurisdictions' discretion to go further than the SORNA minimum is not limited.

C. Retroactivity

The applicability of the SORNA requirements is not limited to sex offenders whose predicate sex offense convictions occur following a jurisdiction's implementation of a conforming registration program. Rather, SORNA's requirements took effect when SORNA was enacted on July 27, 2006, and they have applied since that time to all sex offenders, including those whose convictions predate SORNA's enactment. See 72 FR 8894, 8895-96 (Feb. 28, 2007); 28 CFR 72.3. The application of the SORNA standards to sex offenders whose convictions predate SORNA creates no ex post facto problem "because the SORNA sex offender registration and notification requirements are intended to be non-punitive, regulatory measures adopted for public safety purposes, and hence may validly be applied (and enforced by criminal sanctions) against sex offenders whose predicate convictions occurred prior to the creation of these requirements. See Smith v. Doe, 538 U.S. 84 (2003)." 72 FR at 8896.

As a practical matter, jurisdictions may not be able to identify all sex offenders who fall within the SORNA registration categories, where the predicate convictions predate the enactment of SORNA or the jurisdiction's implementation of the SORNA standards in its registration program, particularly where such sex offenders have left the justice system and merged into the general population long ago. But many sex offenders with such convictions will remain in (or reenter) the system because:

- They are incarcerated or under supervision, either for the predicate sex offense or for some other crime;

- They are already registered or subject to a pre-existing sex offender registration requirement under the jurisdiction's law; or

- They hereafter reenter the jurisdiction's justice system because of conviction for some other crime (whether or not a sex offense).

Sex offenders in these three classes are within the cognizance of the jurisdiction, and the jurisdiction will often have independent reasons to review their criminal histories for penal, correctional, or registration/notification purposes. Accordingly, a jurisdiction will be deemed to have substantially implemented the SORNA standards with respect to sex offenders whose predicate convictions predate the enactment of SORNA or the implementation of SORNA in the jurisdiction's program if it registers these sex offenders, when they fall within any of the three classes described above, in conformity with the SORNA standards. (For more about the registration of sex offenders in these classes, see the discussion under "retroactive classes" in Part IX of these Guidelines.)

The required retroactive application of the SORNA requirements will also be limited in some cases by the limits on the required duration of registration. As discussed in Part XII of these Guidelines, SORNA requires minimum registration periods of varying length for sex offenders in different categories, defined by criteria relating to the nature of their sex offenses and their history of recidivism. This means that a sex offender with a pre-SORNA conviction may have been in the community for a greater amount of time than the registration period required by SORNA. For example, SORNA § 115 requires registration for 25 years for a sex offender whose offense satisfies the "tier II" criteria of section 111(3). A sex offender who was released from imprisonment for such an offense in 1980 is already more than 25 years out from the time of release. In such cases, a jurisdiction may credit the sex offender with the time elapsed from his or her release (or the time elapsed from sentencing, in case of a non-incarcerative sentence), and does not have to require the sex offender to register on the basis of the conviction, even if the criteria for retroactive application of the SORNA standards under this Part are otherwise satisfied.

As with other requirements under SORNA and these Guidelines, the foregoing discussion identifies only the minimum required for SORNA compliance. Jurisdictions are free to require registration for broader classes of sex offenders with convictions that predate SORNA or the jurisdiction's implementation of the SORNA standards in its program.

D. Automation—Electronic Databases and Software

Several features of SORNA contemplate, or will require as a practical matter, the use of current electronic and cyber technology to seamlessly track sex offenders who move from one jurisdiction to another, ensure that information concerning registrants is immediately made available to all interested jurisdictions, and make information concerning sex offenders immediately available to the public as appropriate. These include provisions for immediate information sharing among jurisdictions under SORNA § 113(c); a requirement in section 119(b) that the Attorney General ensure "that updated information about a sex offender is immediately transmitted by electronic forwarding to all relevant jurisdictions"; and requirements in section 121(b) that sex offender registration information and updates thereto be provided immediately to various public and private entities and individuals. (For more about these information sharing requirements and associated time frames, *see* Parts VII.B and X of these Guidelines.)

Carrying out the SORNA information sharing requirements accordingly will entail maintenance by jurisdictions of their registries in the form of electronic databases, whose included information can be electronically transmitted to other jurisdictions and entities. This point is further discussed in connection with the specific SORNA standards, particularly in Parts VI, VII, and X of these Guidelines.

Section 123 of SORNA directs the Attorney General, in consultation with the jurisdictions, to develop and support registry management and website software. The purposes of the software include facilitating the immediate exchange of sex offender information among jurisdictions, public access through the Internet to sex offender information and other forms of community notification, and compliance in other respects with the SORNA requirements. As required by section 123, the Department of Justice will develop and make available to the jurisdictions software tools for the operation of their sex offender registration and notification programs, which will, as far as possible, be designed to automate these processes and enable the jurisdictions to implement SORNA's requirements by utilizing the software.

E. Implementation

Section 124 of SORNA sets a general time frame of three years for implementation, running from the date of enactment of SORNA, i.e., from July 27, 2006. The Attorney General is authorized to provide up to two one-year extensions of this deadline. Failure to comply within the applicable time frame would result in a 10% reduction of federal justice assistance funding under 42 U.S.C. 3750 *et seq.* ("Byrne Justice Assistance Grant" funding). *See* SORNA § 125(a). Funding withheld from jurisdictions because of noncompliance would be reallocated to other jurisdictions that are in compliance, or could be reallocated to the noncompliant jurisdiction to be used solely for the purpose of SORNA implementation.

While SORNA sets minimum standards for jurisdictions' registration and notification programs, it does not require that its standards be implemented by statute. Hence, in assessing compliance with SORNA, the totality of a jurisdiction's rules governing the operation of its registration and notification program will be considered, including administrative policies and procedures as well as statutes.

The SMART Office will be responsible for determining whether a jurisdiction has substantially implemented the SORNA requirements. The affected jurisdictions are encouraged to submit information to the SMART Office concerning existing and proposed sex offender registration and notification provisions with as much lead time as possible, so the SMART Office can assess the adequacy of existing or proposed measures to implement the SORNA requirements and work with the submitting jurisdictions to overcome any shortfalls or problems. At the latest, submissions establishing compliance with the SORNA requirements should be made to the SMART Office at least three months before the deadline date of July 27, 2009—i.e., by April 27, 2009—so that the matter can be determined before the Byrne Grant funding reduction required by SORNA § 125 for noncompliant jurisdictions takes effect. If it is anticipated that a submitting jurisdiction may need an extension of time as described in SORNA § 124(b), the submission to the SMART Office—which should be made by April 27, 2009, as noted—should include a description of the jurisdiction's implementation efforts and an explanation why an extension is needed.

SORNA § 125 refers to "substantial" implementation of SORNA. The standard of "substantial implementation" is satisfied with respect to an element of the SORNA requirements if a jurisdiction carries out the requirements of SORNA as interpreted and explained in these Guidelines. Hence, the standard is satisfied if a jurisdiction implements measures that these Guidelines identify as sufficient to implement (or "substantially" implement) the SORNA requirements.

Jurisdictions' programs cannot be approved as substantially implementing the SORNA requirements if they substitute some basically different approach to sex offender registration and notification that does not incorporate SORNA's baseline requirements—e.g., a "risk assessment" approach that broadly authorizes the waiver of registration or notification requirements or their reduction below the minima specified in SORNA on the basis of factors that SORNA does not authorize as grounds for waiving or limiting registration or notification. Likewise, the "substantial implementation" standard does not mean that programs can be approved if they dispense wholesale with categorical requirements set forth in SORNA, such as by adopting general standards that do not require registration for offenses included in SORNA's offense coverage provisions, that set regular reporting periods for changes in registration information that are longer than those specified in SORNA, or that prescribe less frequent appearances for verification or shorter registration periods than SORNA requires.

The substantial implementation standard does, however, contemplate that there is some latitude to approve a jurisdiction's implementation efforts, even if they do not exactly follow in all respects the specifications of SORNA or these Guidelines. For example, section 116 of SORNA requires periodic in-person appearances by sex offenders to verify their registration information. But in some cases this will be impossible, either temporarily (e.g., in the case of a sex offender hospitalized and unconscious because of an injury at the time of the scheduled appearance) or permanently (e.g., in the case of a sex offender who is in a persistent vegetative state). In other cases, the appearance may not be literally impossible, but there may be reasons to allow some relaxation of the requirement in light of the sex offender's personal circumstances. For example, a sex offender may unexpectedly need to deal with a family emergency at the time of a scheduled appearance, where failure to make the appearance will mean not verifying the registration information within the exact time frame specified by SORNA § 116. A jurisdiction may wish to authorize rescheduling of the appearance in such cases. Doing so would not necessarily undermine substantially the objectives of the SORNA verification requirements, so long as the jurisdiction's rules or procedures require that the sex offender notify the official responsible for monitoring the sex offender of the difficulty, and that the appearance promptly be carried out once the interfering circumstance is resolved.

In general, the SMART Office will consider on a case-by-case basis whether jurisdictions' rules or procedures that do not exactly follow the provisions of SORNA or these Guidelines "substantially" implement SORNA, assessing whether the departure from a SORNA requirement will or will not substantially disserve the objectives of the requirement. If a jurisdiction is relying on the authorization to approve measures that "substantially" implement SORNA as the basis for an element or elements in its system that depart in some respect from the exact requirements of SORNA or these Guidelines, the jurisdiction's submission to the SMART Office should identify these elements and explain why the departure from the SORNA requirements should not be considered a failure to substantially implement SORNA.

Beyond the general standard of substantial implementation, SORNA § 125(b) includes special provisions for cases in which the highest court of a jurisdiction has held that the jurisdiction's constitution is in some respect in conflict with the SORNA requirements. If a jurisdiction believes that it faces such a situation, it should inform the SMART Office. The SMART Office will then work with the jurisdiction to see whether the problem can be overcome, as the statute provides. If it is not possible to overcome the problem, then the SMART Office may approve the jurisdiction's adoption of reasonable alternative measures that are consistent with the purposes of SORNA.

Section 125 of SORNA, as discussed above, provides for a funding reduction for jurisdictions that do not substantially implement SORNA within the applicable time frame. Section 126 of SORNA authorizes positive funding assistance—the Sex Offender Management Assistance ("SOMA") grant program—to all registration jurisdictions to help offset the costs of SORNA implementation, with enhanced payments authorized for jurisdictions that effect such implementation within one or two years of SORNA's enactment. Congress has not appropriated funding for the SOMA program at the time of the issuance of these Guidelines. If funding for this program is forthcoming in the future, additional guidance will be provided concerning application for grants under the program.

III.   COVERED JURISDICTIONS

Section 112(a) of SORNA states that "[e]ach jurisdiction shall maintain a jurisdiction-wide sex offender registry conforming to the requirements of this title," and section 124 provides specific deadlines for "jurisdictions" to carry out the SORNA implementation. Related definitions appear in section 111(9) and (10). Section 111(9) provides that "sex offender registry" means a registry of sex offenders and a notification program.

Section 111(10) provides that "jurisdiction" refers to:

• the 50 States;

- the District of Columbia;

- the five principal U.S. territories—the Commonwealth of Puerto Rico, Guam, American Samoa, the Northern Mariana Islands, and the United States Virgin Islands; and

- Indian tribes to the extent provided in section 127.

Some of the provisions in SORNA are formulated as directions to sex offenders, including those appearing in sections 113(a)-(b), 113(c) (first sentence), 114(a), 115(a), and 116. Other SORNA provisions are cast as directions to jurisdictions or their officials, such as those appearing in sections 113(c) (second sentence), 113(e), 114(b), 117(a), 118, 121(b), and 122. To meet the requirement under sections 112 and 124 that covered jurisdictions must implement SORNA in their registration and notification programs, each jurisdiction must incorporate in the laws and rules governing its registration and notification program the requirements that SORNA imposes on sex offenders, as well as those that are addressed directly to jurisdictions and their officials.

While the "jurisdictions" assigned sex offender registration and notification responsibilities by SORNA are the 50 States, the District of Columbia, the principal territories, and Indian tribes (to the extent provided in section 127), as described above, this does not limit the ability of these jurisdictions to carry out these functions through their political subdivisions or other entities within the jurisdiction. For example, a jurisdiction may assign responsibility for initially registering sex offenders upon their release from imprisonment to correctional personnel who are employees of the jurisdiction's government, but the responsibility for continued tracking and registration of sex offenders thereafter may be assigned to personnel of local police departments, sheriffs' offices, or supervision agencies who are municipal employees. Moreover, in carrying out their registration and notification functions, jurisdictions are free to utilize (and to allow their agencies and political subdivisions to utilize) entities and individuals who may not be governmental agencies or employees in a narrow sense, such as contractors, volunteers, and community-based organizations that are capable of discharging these functions. SORNA does not limit jurisdictions' discretion concerning such matters. Rather, so long as a jurisdiction's laws and rules provide consistently for the discharge of the required registration and notification functions by some responsible individuals or entities, the specifics concerning such assignments of responsibility are matters within the jurisdiction's discretion. References in these Guidelines should be understood accordingly, so that (for example) a reference to an "official" carrying out a registration function does not mean that the function must be carried out by a government employee, but rather is simply a way of referring to whatever individual is assigned responsibility for the function.

With respect to Indian tribes, SORNA recognizes that tribes may vary in their capacities and preferences regarding the discharge of sex offender registration and notification functions, and accordingly section 127 of SORNA has special provisions governing the treatment of Indian tribes as registration jurisdictions or the delegation of registration and notification functions to the states. Specifically, section 127(a)(1) generally afforded federally recognized Indian tribes a choice between electing to carry out the sex offender registration and notification functions specified in SORNA in relation to sex offenders subject to its jurisdiction, or delegating those functions to a state or states within which the tribe is located. SORNA provided a period of one year commencing with SORNA's enactment on July 27, 2006 for tribes to make this choice. SORNA further required that the election to become a SORNA registration jurisdiction, or to delegate to a state or states, be made by resolution or other enactment of the tribal council or comparable governmental body. Hence, the decision must have been made by a tribal governmental entity—"the tribal council or comparable governmental body"—that has the legal authority to make binding legislative decisions for the tribe. (However, delegation to the state or states is automatic for a tribe subject to state law enforcement jurisdiction under 18 U.S.C. 1162, and for a tribe that did not affirmatively elect to become a SORNA registration jurisdiction on or prior to July 27, 2007—see the discussion of section 127(a)(2) below.)

If a tribe has elected to be a SORNA registration jurisdiction in conformity with section 127, its functions and responsibilities regarding sex offender registration and notification are the same as those of a state. Duplication of registration and notification functions by tribes and states is not required, however, and such tribes may enter into cooperative agreements with the states for the discharge of these functions, as discussed below in connection with section 127(b).

If a tribe has elected to delegate to a state—or if a delegation to the state occurs pursuant to section 127(a)(2)—then the state is fully responsible for carrying out the SORNA registration and notification functions, and the delegation includes an undertaking by the tribe to "provide access to its territory and such other cooperation and assistance as may be needed to enable [the state] to carry out and enforce the requirements of [SORNA]." SORNA § 127(a)(1)(B). This does not mean, however, that tribal authorities in such a tribe are precluded from carrying out sex offender registration and notification functions. Sovereign powers that these tribes otherwise possess to prescribe registration and notification requirements for sex offenders subject to their jurisdiction are not restricted by SORNA, so long as there is no conflict with the state's discharge of its responsibilities under SORNA. Moreover, as discussed above, states generally have discretion concerning the entities within the state through which the SORNA registration and notification functions are to be carried out, and tribal entities are not excluded. For example, with respect to a tribe subject to state law enforcement jurisdiction under 18 U.S.C. 1162, the state may conclude that a tribal agency is best situated to carry out registration functions with respect to sex offenders residing in the tribe's territory. In some instances such tribes may have been operating sex offender registration programs of their own prior to the enactment of SORNA, and arranging with the tribe for the continued discharge of registration functions by the tribal authorities may be the most expedient way for the state to carry out the required SORNA functions in such a tribal area.

Section 127(a)(2) of SORNA specifies three circumstances in which registration and notification functions are deemed to be delegated to the state or states in which a tribe is located, even if the tribe did not make an affirmative decision to delegate:

- Under subparagraph (A) of subsection (a)(2), these functions are always delegated to the state if the tribe is subject to the law enforcement jurisdiction of the state under 18 U.S.C. 1162. (If a tribe's land is in part subject to state law enforcement jurisdiction under 18

U.S.C. 1162 and in part outside of the areas subject to 18 U.S.C. 1162, then: (i) sex offender registration and notification functions are automatically delegated to the relevant state in the portion of the tribal land subject to 18 U.S.C. 1162, and (ii) the tribe could have made an election between functioning as a registration jurisdiction or delegating registration and notification functions to the state in the portion of its land that is not subject to 18 U.S.C. 1162.)

- Under subparagraph (B) of subsection (a)(2), these functions are delegated to the state or states if the tribe did not make an affirmative election to function as a registration jurisdiction within one year of the enactment of SORNA—i.e., within one year of July 27, 2006—or rescinds a previous election to function as a registration jurisdiction.

- Under subparagraph (C) of subsection (a)(2), these functions are delegated to the state or states if the Attorney General determines that the tribe has not substantially implemented the requirements of SORNA and is not likely to become capable of doing so within a reasonable amount time.

If a tribe did elect under section 127 to become a SORNA registration jurisdiction, section 127(b) specifies that this does not mean that the tribe must duplicate registration and notification functions that are fully carried out by the state or states within which the tribe is located, and subsection (b) further authorizes the tribes and the states to make cooperative arrangements for the discharge of some or all of these functions. For example, SORNA § 118 requires jurisdictions to make information concerning their sex offenders available to the public through the Internet. If a tribe did not want to maintain a separate sex offender website for this purpose, it would not need to do so, as long as a cooperative agreement was made with the state to have information concerning the tribe's registrants posted on the state's sex offender website. Likewise, a tribe that has elected to be a SORNA registration jurisdiction remains free to make cooperative agreements under which the state (or a political subdivision thereof) will handle registration of the tribe's sex offenders—such as initially registering these sex offenders, conducting periodic appearances of the sex offenders to verify the registration information, and receiving reports by the sex offenders concerning changes in the registration information—to the extent and in a manner mutually agreeable to the tribe and the state. In general, the use of cooperative agreements affords tribes flexibility in deciding which functions under SORNA they would seek to have state authorities perform, and which they wish to control or discharge directly. For example, the state could carry out certain registration functions, but the tribe could retain jurisdiction over the arrest within its territory of sex offenders who fail to register, update registrations, or make required verification appearances, if a cooperative agreement between the tribe and the state so provided.

Tribes that have elected to be SORNA registration jurisdictions in conformity with section 127 may also make agreements or enter into arrangements with other such tribes for the cooperative or shared discharge of registration and notification functions. For example, a group of tribes with adjacent territories might wish to enter into an agreement under which the participating tribes contribute resources and information to the extent of their capacities, but the tribal police department (or some other agency) of one of the tribes in the group has primary responsibility for the discharge of the SORNA registration functions in relation to sex offenders subject to the jurisdiction of any of the tribes in the group—such as initially registering sex offenders who enter the jurisdiction of any of the tribes, receiving information from those sex offenders concerning subsequent changes in residence or other registration information, and conducting periodic in-person appearances by the registrants to verify and update the registration information, as SORNA requires. Likewise, with respect to maintenance of websites providing public access to sex offender information, as required by SORNA § 118, tribes could enter into agreements or arrangements among themselves for the shared administration or operation of websites covering the sex offenders of the participating tribes. So long as such agreements or arrangements among tribes are designed to ensure that the SORNA registration and notification functions are carried out consistently in relation to sex offenders subject to the jurisdiction of any of the participating tribes, discharge of the SORNA responsibilities by such means will be considered as satisfying the SORNA substantial implementation standard.

IV.   COVERED SEX OFFENSES AND SEX OFFENDERS

SORNA refers to the persons required to register under its standards as "sex offenders," and section 111(1) of SORNA defines "sex offender" in the relevant sense to mean "an individual who was convicted of a sex offense." "Sex offense" is in turn defined in section 111(5) and related provisions. The term encompasses a broad range of offenses of a sexual nature under the law of any jurisdiction—including offenses under federal, military, state, territorial, local, tribal, and foreign law, but with some qualification regarding foreign convictions as discussed below.

A. Convictions Generally

A "sex offender" as defined in SORNA § 111(1) is a person who was "convicted" of a sex offense. Hence, whether an individual has a sex offense "conviction" determines whether he or she is within the minimum categories for which the SORNA standards require registration.

Because the SORNA registration requirements are predicated on convictions, registration (or continued registration) is normally not required under the SORNA standards if the predicate conviction is reversed, vacated, or set aside, or if the person is pardoned for the offense on the ground of innocence. This does not mean, however, that nominal changes or terminological variations that do not relieve a conviction of substantive effect negate the SORNA requirements. For example, the need to require registration would not be avoided by a jurisdiction's having a procedure under which the convictions of sex offenders in certain categories (e.g., young adult sex offenders who satisfy certain criteria) are referred to as something other than "convictions," or under which the convictions of such sex offenders may nominally be "vacated" or "set aside," but the sex offender is nevertheless required to serve what amounts to a criminal sentence for the offense. Rather, an adult sex offender is "convicted" for SORNA purposes if the sex offender remains subject to penal consequences based on the conviction, however it may be styled. Likewise, the sealing of a criminal record or other action that limits the publicity or availability of a conviction, but does not deprive it of continuing legal validity, does not change its status as a "conviction" for purposes of SORNA.

"Convictions" for SORNA purposes include convictions of juveniles who are prosecuted as adults. It does not include juvenile delinquency adjudications, except under the circumstances specified in SORNA § 111(8). Section 111(8) provides that delinquency adjudications count as convictions "only if the offender is 14 years of age or older at the time of the offense and the offense adjudicated was comparable to or more severe than aggravated sexual abuse (as described in section 2241 of title 18, United States Code), or was an attempt or conspiracy to commit such an offense."

Hence, SORNA does not require registration for juveniles adjudicated delinquent for all sex offenses for which an adult sex offender would be required to register, but rather requires registration only for a defined class of older juveniles who are adjudicated delinquent for committing particularly serious sexually assaultive crimes (or attempts or conspiracies to commit such crimes). Considering the relevant aspects of the federal "aggravated sexual abuse" offense referenced in section 111(8), it suffices for substantial implementation if a jurisdiction applies SORNA's requirements to juveniles at least 14 years old at the time of the offense who are adjudicated delinquent for committing (or attempting or conspiring to commit) offenses under laws that cover:

- engaging in a sexual act with another by force or the threat of serious violence; or

- engaging in a sexual act with another by rendering unconscious or involuntarily drugging the victim.

"Sexual act" for this purpose should be understood to include any degree of genital or anal penetration, and any oral-genital or oral-anal contact. This follows from the relevant portions of the definition of sexual act in 18 U.S.C. 2246(2), which applies to the 18 U.S.C. 2241 "aggravated sexual abuse" offense. (The summary of comments received on these Guidelines as initially proposed for public comment may be consulted for further explanation concerning this understanding of the requirements for substantial implementation of section 111(8).)

As with other aspects of SORNA, the foregoing defines minimum standards. Hence, the inclusions and exclusions in the definition of "conviction" for purposes of SORNA do not constrain jurisdictions from requiring registration by additional individuals—e.g., more broadly defined categories of juveniles adjudicated delinquent for sex offenses—if they are so inclined.

B. Foreign Convictions

Section 111(5)(B) of SORNA instructs that registration need not be required on the basis of a foreign conviction if the conviction "was not obtained with sufficient safeguards for fundamental fairness and due process for the accused under guidelines or regulations established [by the Attorney General]." The following standards are adopted pursuant to section 111(5)(B):

- Sex offense convictions under the laws of Canada, United Kingdom, Australia, and New Zealand are deemed to have been obtained with sufficient safeguards for fundamental fairness and due process, and registration must be required for such convictions on the same footing as domestic convictions.

- Sex offense convictions under the laws of any foreign country are deemed to have been obtained with sufficient safeguards for fundamental fairness and due process if the U.S. State Department, in its Country Reports on Human Rights Practices, has concluded that an independent judiciary generally (or vigorously) enforced the right to a fair trial in that country during the year in which the conviction occurred. Registration must be required on the basis of such convictions on the same footing as domestic convictions.

- With respect to sex offense convictions in foreign countries that do not satisfy the criteria stated above, a jurisdiction is not required to register the convicted person if the jurisdiction determines—through whatever process or procedure it may choose to adopt—that the conviction does not constitute a reliable indication of factual guilt because of the lack of an impartial tribunal, because of denial of the right to respond to the evidence against the person or to present exculpatory evidence, or because of denial of the right to the assistance of counsel.

The foregoing standards do not mean that jurisdictions must incorporate these particular criteria or procedures into their registration systems. Jurisdictions may wish to register all foreign sex offense convicts, or to register such convicts with fewer qualifications or limitations than those allowed under the standards set forth above. The stated criteria only define the minimum categories of foreign convicts for whom registration is required for compliance with SORNA, and as is generally the case under SORNA, jurisdictions are free to require registration more broadly than the SORNA minimum.

C. Sex Offenses Generally

The general definition of sex offenses for which registration is required under the SORNA standards appears in section 111(5)(A). The clauses in the definition cover the following categories of offenses:

- SEXUAL ACT AND SEXUAL CONTACT OFFENSES (§ 111(5)(A)(i)): The first clause in the definition covers "a criminal offense that has an element involving a sexual act or sexual contact with another." ("Criminal offense" in the relevant sense refers to offenses under any body of criminal law, including state, local, tribal, foreign, military, and other offenses, as provided in section 111(6).) The offenses covered by this clause should be understood to include all sexual offenses whose elements involve: (i) any type or degree of genital, oral, or anal penetration, or (ii) any sexual touching of or contact with a person's body, either directly or through the clothing. *Cf.* 18 U.S.C. 2246(2)-(3) (federal law definitions of sexual act and sexual contact).

- SPECIFIED OFFENSES AGAINST MINORS (§ 111(5)(A)(ii)): The second clause in the definition covers "a criminal offense that is a specified offense against a minor." The statute provides a detailed definition of "specified offense against a minor" in section 111(7), which is discussed separately below.

- SPECIFIED FEDERAL OFFENSES (§ 111(5)(A)(iii)): The third clause covers most sexual offenses under federal law. The clause identifies chapters and offense provisions in the federal criminal code by citation.

- SPECIFIED MILITARY OFFENSES (§ 111(5)(A)(iv)): The fourth clause covers sex offenses under the Uniform Code of Military Justice, as specified by the Secretary of Defense.

- ATTEMPTS AND CONSPIRACIES (§ 111(5)(A)(v)): The final clause in the definition covers attempts and conspiracies to commit offenses that are otherwise covered by the definition of "sex offenses." This includes both offenses prosecuted under general attempt or conspiracy provisions, where the object offense falls under the SORNA "sex offense" definition, and particular offenses that are defined as, or in substance amount to, attempts or conspiracies to commit offenses that are otherwise covered. For example, in the latter category, a jurisdiction may define an offense of "assault with intent to commit rape." Whether or not the word "attempt" is used in the definition of the offense, this is in substance an offense that covers certain attempts to commit rapes and hence is covered under the final clause of the SORNA definition.

SORNA § 111(5)(C) qualifies the foregoing definition of "sex offense" to exclude "[a]n offense involving consensual sexual conduct . . . if the victim was an adult, unless the adult was under the custodial authority of the offender at the time of the offense, or if the victim was at least 13 years old and the offender was not more than 4 years older than the victim." The general exclusion with respect to consensual sexual offenses involving adult victims means, for example, that a jurisdiction does not have to require registration based on prostitution offenses that consist of the offender paying or receiving payment from an adult for a sexual act between them (unless the victim is under the custodial authority of the offender). The exclusion for certain cases involving child victims based on victim age and age difference means that a jurisdiction may not have to require registration in some cases based on convictions under provisions that prohibit sexual acts or contact (even if consensual) with underage persons. For example, under the laws of some jurisdictions, an 18-year-old may be criminally liable for engaging in consensual sex with a 15-year-old. The jurisdiction would not have to require registration in such a case to comply with the SORNA standards, since the victim was at least 13 and the offender was not more than four years older.

D. Specified Offenses Against Minors

The offenses for which registration is required under the SORNA standards include any "specified offense against a minor" as defined in section 111(7). The SORNA § 111(7) definition of specified offense against a minor covers any offense against a minor—i.e., a person under the age of 18, as provided in section 111(14)—that involves any of the following:

- KIDNAPPING OR FALSE IMPRISONMENT OF A MINOR (§ 111(7)(A)-(B)): These clauses cover "[a]n offense (unless committed by a parent or guardian) involving kidnapping [of a minor]" and "[a]n offense (unless committed by a parent or guardian) involving false imprisonment [of a minor]." The relevant offenses are those whose gravamen is abduction or unlawful restraint of a person, which go by different names in different jurisdictions, such as "kidnapping," "criminal restraint," or "false imprisonment." Jurisdictions can implement the offense coverage requirement of these clauses by requiring registration for persons convicted of offenses of this type (however designated) whose victims were below the age of 18. It is left to jurisdictions' discretion under these clauses whether registration should be required for such offenses in cases where the offender is a parent or guardian of the victim.

- SOLICITATION OF A MINOR TO ENGAGE IN SEXUAL CONDUCT (§ 111(7)(C)): This clause covers "[s]olicitation [of a minor] to engage in sexual conduct." "Solicitation" under this clause and other SORNA provisions that use the term should be understood broadly to include any direction, request, enticement, persuasion, or encouragement of a minor to engage in sexual conduct. "Sexual conduct" should be understood to refer to any sexual activity involving physical contact. (See the discussion later in this list of "criminal sexual conduct" under section 111(7)(H).) Hence, jurisdictions can implement the offense coverage requirement under this clause by requiring registration, in cases where the victim was below the age of 18, based on:

  o any conviction for an offense involving solicitation of the victim under a general attempt or solicitation provision, where the elements of the object offense include sexual activity involving physical contact, and

  o any conviction for an offense involving solicitation of the victim under any provision defining a particular crime whose elements include soliciting or attempting to engage in sexual activity involving physical contact.

- USE OF A MINOR IN A SEXUAL PERFORMANCE (§ 111(7)(D)): This clause covers offenses involving "[u]se [of a minor] in a sexual performance." That includes both live performances and using minors in the production of pornography, and has some overlap with section 111(7)(G), which expressly covers child pornography offenses.

- SOLICITATION OF A MINOR TO PRACTICE PROSTITUTION (§ 111(7)(E)): This clause covers offenses involving "[s]olicitation [of a minor] to practice prostitution." Jurisdictions can implement the offense coverage requirement under this clause by requiring registration, in cases where the victim was below the age of 18, based on:

  o any conviction for an offense involving solicitation of the victim under a general attempt or solicitation provision, where the object offense is a prostitution offense, and

  o any conviction for an offense involving solicitation of the victim under any provision defining a particular crime whose elements include soliciting or attempting to get a person to engage in prostitution.

- VIDEO VOYEURISM INVOLVING A MINOR (§ 111(7)(F)): This clause covers "[v]ideo voyeurism as described in section 1801 of title 18, United States Code [against a minor]." The cited federal offense in essence covers capturing the image of a private area of another person's body, where the victim has a reasonable expectation of privacy against such conduct. Jurisdictions can implement the offense coverage requirement under this clause by requiring registration for offenses of this type, in cases where the victim was below the age of 18.

- POSSESSION, PRODUCTION, OR DISTRIBUTION OF CHILD PORNOGRAPHY (§ 111(7)(G)): This clause covers "possession, production, or distribution of child pornography." Jurisdictions can implement the offense coverage requirement under this clause by requiring registration for offenses whose gravamen is creating or participating in the creation of sexually explicit visual depictions of persons below the age of 18, making such depictions available to others, or having or receiving such depictions.

- CRIMINAL SEXUAL CONDUCT INVOLVING A MINOR AND RELATED INTERNET ACTIVITIES (§ 111(7)(H)): This clause covers "[c]riminal sexual conduct involving a minor, or the use of the Internet to facilitate or attempt such conduct." The definition has two parts:

  ○ The "criminal sexual conduct involving a minor" language in this definition covers sexual offenses whose elements involve physical contact with the victim—such as provisions defining crimes of "rape," "sexual assault," "sexual abuse," or "incest"—in cases where the victim was below 18 at the time of the offense. In addition, it covers offenses whose elements involve using other persons in prostitution—such as provisions defining crimes of "pandering," "procuring," or "pimping"—in cases where the victim was below 18 at the time of the offense. Coverage is not limited to cases where the victim's age is an element of the offense, such as prosecution for specially defined child molestation or child prostitution offenses. Jurisdictions can implement the offense coverage requirement under the "criminal sexual conduct involving a minor" language of this clause by requiring registration for "criminal sexual conduct" offenses as described above whenever the victim was in fact below the age of 18 at the time of the offense. (Section 111(7)(C) and (E) separately require coverage of offenses involving solicitation of a minor to engage in sexual conduct or to practice prostitution, but registration must be required for offenses involving sexual conduct with a minor or the use of a minor in prostitution in light of section 111(7)(H), whether or not the offense involves "solicitation" of the victim.)

  ○ Jurisdictions can implement the "use of the Internet to facilitate or attempt such conduct" part of this definition by requiring registration for offenses that involve use of the Internet in furtherance of criminal sexual conduct involving a minor as defined above, such as attempting to lure minors through Internet communications for the purpose of sexual activity.

- CONDUCT BY ITS NATURE A SEX OFFENSE AGAINST A MINOR (§ 111(7)(I)): The final clause covers "[a]ny conduct that by its nature is a sex offense against a minor." It is intended to ensure coverage of convictions under statutes defining sexual offenses in which the status of the victim as a minor is an element of an offense, such as specially defined child molestation or child prostitution offenses, and other offenses prohibiting sexual activity with underage persons. Jurisdictions can comply with the offense coverage requirement under this clause by including convictions for such offenses in their registration requirements.

E. Protected Witnesses

The requirement that jurisdictions substantially implement SORNA does not preclude their taking measures needed to protect the security of individuals who have been provided new identities and relocated under the federal witness security program (*see* 18 U.S.C. 3521 *et seq.*) or under other comparable witness security programs operated by non-federal jurisdictions. A jurisdiction may conclude that it is necessary to exclude an individual afforded protection in such a program from its sex offender registry or from public notification for security reasons, though the individual otherwise satisfies the criteria for registration and notification under SORNA. Alternatively, the jurisdiction may choose not to waive registration but may identify the registrant in the registration system records only by his or her new identity or data, if such modifications can be so devised that they are not transparent and do not permit the registrant's original identity or participation in a witness security program to be inferred. Jurisdictions are permitted and encouraged to make provision in their laws and procedures to accommodate consideration of the security of such individuals and to honor requests from the United States Marshals Service and other agencies responsible for witness protection in order to ensure that their original identities are not compromised.

With respect to witnesses afforded federal protection, 18 U.S.C. 3521(b)(1)(H) specifically authorizes the Attorney General to "protect the confidentiality of the identity and location of persons subject to registration requirements as convicted offenders under Federal or State law, including prescribing alternative procedures to those otherwise provided by Federal or State law for registration and tracking of such persons." U.S. Department of Justice Witness Security Program officials accordingly determine on a case-by-case basis whether such witnesses will be required to register, and if registration occurs, whether it will utilize new identities, modified data, or other special conditions or procedures that are warranted to avoid jeopardizing the safety of the protected witnesses.

V.   CLASSES OF SEX OFFENDERS

Section 111(2)-(4) of SORNA defines three "tiers" of sex offenders. The tier classifications have implications in three areas: (i) under section 115, the required duration of registration depends primarily on the tier; (ii) under section 116, the required frequency of in-person appearances by sex offenders to verify registration information depends on the tier; and (iii) under section 118(c)(1), information about tier I sex offenders convicted of offenses other than specified offenses against a minor may be exempted from website disclosure.

21

The use of the "tier" classifications in SORNA relates to substance, not form or terminology. Thus, to implement the SORNA requirements, jurisdictions do not have to label their sex offenders as "tier I," "tier II," and "tier III," and do not have to adopt any other particular approach to labeling or categorization of sex offenders. Rather, the SORNA requirements are met so long as sex offenders who satisfy the SORNA criteria for placement in a particular tier are consistently subject to at least the duration of registration, frequency of in-person appearances for verification, and extent of website disclosure that SORNA requires for that tier.

For example, suppose that a jurisdiction decides to subject all sex offenders to lifetime registration, quarterly verification appearances, and full website posting as described in Part VII of these Guidelines. That would meet the SORNA requirements with respect to sex offenders satisfying the "tier III" criteria, and exceed the minimum required by SORNA with respect to sex offenders satisfying the "tier II" or "tier I" criteria. Hence, such a jurisdiction would be able to implement the SORNA requirements with respect to all sex offenders without any labeling or categorization, and without having to assess individual registrants against the tier criteria in the SORNA definitions. Likewise, any other approach a jurisdiction may devise is acceptable if it ensures that sex offenders satisfying the criteria for each SORNA tier are subject to duration of registration, appearance frequency, and website disclosure requirements that meet or exceed those SORNA requires for the tier.

Turning to the specific tier definitions, SORNA § 111(2) defines "tier I sex offender" to mean "a sex offender other than a tier II or tier III sex offender." Thus, tier I is a residual class that includes all sex offenders who do not satisfy the criteria for tier II or tier III. For example, tier I includes a sex offender whose registration offense is not punishable by imprisonment for more than one year, a sex offender whose registration offense is the receipt or possession of child pornography, and a sex offender whose registration offense is a sexual assault against an adult that involves sexual contact but not a completed or attempted sexual act. (With respect to the last-mentioned category, a sexual assault involving a completed or attempted sexual act would generally result in a tier III classification, as discussed below in connection with SORNA § 111(4)(A)(i)), but the offense coverage specifications for tier II and tier III do not otherwise provide a basis for higher classification of sexual contact or touching offenses involving adult victims.)

The definitions of tier II and tier III—in section 111(3) and 111(4) respectively—are both limited to cases in which the offense for which the sex offender is required to register "is punishable by imprisonment for more than 1 year." This means that the statutory maximum penalty possible for the offense exceeds one year. It does not mean that inclusion in these tiers is limited to cases in which the sex offender is actually sentenced to more than a year of imprisonment.

Because the definitions of tier II and tier III are limited to certain offenses punishable by imprisonment for more than one year, and federal law does not permit imprisonment for more than one year based on Indian tribal court convictions, all tribal court convictions are tier I offenses. However, sex offenses prosecuted in tribal courts may be serious crimes that would typically carry higher penalties if prosecuted in non-tribal jurisdictions. As the incidents of the tier classifications under SORNA only define minimum standards, tribal jurisdictions and other jurisdictions are free to premise more extensive registration and notification requirements on tribal court convictions than the minimum SORNA requires for tier I offenders, and may wish to do so considering the substantive nature of the offense or other factors.

Regardless of which jurisdiction convicts the sex offender, the requirements with respect to the potential length of imprisonment under the statute relate to individual offenses rather than to aggregate penalties. For example, suppose that a sex offender is charged in three counts with the commission of sex offenses each of which is punishable by at most one year of imprisonment, and upon conviction is sentenced to three consecutive terms of six months of incarceration. Though the aggregate penalty is 18 months, these convictions do not place the sex offender above tier I, because each offense was not punishable by more than one year of imprisonment.

The classification of sex offenders as tier II or tier III under SORNA depends in part on the nature of the offense for which the sex offender is required to register. In assessing whether the offense satisfies the criteria for tier II or tier III classification, jurisdictions generally may premise the determination on the elements of the offense, and are not required to look to underlying conduct that is not reflected in the offense of conviction. However, where the tier classification depends on commission of an offense against a victim who is below a certain age, the requirement to give weight to this factor (victim age) is not limited to cases involving convictions for offenses whose elements specify that the victim must be below that age. Rather, the requirement applies as well in cases in which the offender is convicted of a more generally defined offense that may be committed against victims of varying ages, if the victim was in fact below the relevant age. For example, in a case in which the sex offender was convicted of a generally defined "sexual contact" offense, whose elements include no specification as to victim age, tier II treatment is required if the victim was in fact below 18 (SORNA § 111(3)(A)(iv)), and tier III treatment is required if the victim was in fact below 13 (SORNA § 111(4)(A)(ii)).

Beyond the requirement of an offense punishable by imprisonment for more than one year, the specific offense-related criteria for tier II are that the registration offense falls within one of two lists. In general terms, these lists cover most sexual abuse or exploitation offenses against minors. (Here as elsewhere in SORNA, "minor" means a person under the age of 18—see SORNA § 111(14).) The first list, appearing in section 111(3)(A), covers offenses committed against minors that are comparable to or more severe than a number of cited federal offenses—those under 18 U.S.C. 1591, 2422(b), 2423(a), and 2244—and attempts and conspiracies to commit such offenses. The second list, appearing in section 111(3)(B), covers use of a minor in a sexual performance, solicitation of a minor to practice prostitution, and production or distribution of child pornography. Determining whether a jurisdiction's offenses satisfy the criteria for this tier is simplified by recognizing that the various cited and described offenses essentially cover:

- offenses involving the use of minors in prostitution, and inchoate or preparatory offenses (including attempts, conspiracies, and solicitations) that are directed to the commission of such offenses;

- offenses against minors involving sexual contact—i.e., any sexual touching of or contact with the intimate parts of the body, either directly or through the clothing—and inchoate or preparatory offenses (including attempts, conspiracies, and solicitations) that are directed to the commission of such offenses;

- offenses involving use of a minor in a sexual performance; and

- offenses involving the production or distribution of child pornography, i.e., offenses whose gravamen is creating or participating in the creation of sexually explicit visual depictions of minors or making such depictions available to others.

Hence, jurisdictions can implement the relevant SORNA requirements by according "tier II" treatment to sex offenders convicted of offenses of these four types.

The corresponding offense coverage specifications for "tier III" in section 111(4)(A)-(B) cover offenses punishable by more than one year of imprisonment in the following categories:

- Offenses comparable to or more severe than aggravated sexual abuse or sexual abuse as described in 18 U.S.C. 2241 and 2242, or an attempt or conspiracy to commit such an offense (*see* SORNA § 111(4)(A)(i)). Considering the definitions of the cited federal offenses, comparable offenses under the laws of other jurisdictions would be those that cover:

  o   engaging in a sexual act with another by force or threat (*see* 18 U.S.C. 2241(a), 2242(1));

  o   engaging in a sexual act with another who has been rendered unconscious or involuntarily drugged, or who is otherwise incapable of appraising the nature of the conduct or declining to participate (*see* 18 U.S.C. 2241(b), 2242(2)); or

  o   engaging in a sexual act with a child under the age of 12 (*see* 18 U.S.C. 2241(c)).

  Considering the related definition in 18 U.S.C. 2246(2), "sexual act" for this purpose would include: (i) oral-genital or oral-anal contact, (ii) any degree of genital or anal penetration, and (iii) direct genital touching of a child under the age of 16.

- Offenses against a minor below the age of 13 that are comparable to or more severe than abusive sexual contact as defined in 18 U.S.C. 2244, or an attempt or conspiracy to commit such an offense (*see* SORNA § 111(4)(A)(ii)). Considering the definitions of the federal offenses in 18 U.S.C. 2244 and the related definition in 18 U.S.C. 2246(3), comparable offenses under the laws of other jurisdictions would be those that cover sexual touching of or contact with the intimate parts of the body, either directly or through the clothing, where the victim is under 13.

- Kidnapping of a minor (unless committed by a parent or guardian).

Hence, jurisdictions can implement the relevant SORNA requirements by according "tier III" treatment to sex offenders convicted of offenses of these three types.

In addition to including criteria relating to the nature of the registration offense, the definitions of tier II and tier III accord significance to a registrant's history of recidivism. Specifically, section 111(3)(C) places in tier II any sex offender whose registration offense is punishable by imprisonment for more than one year, where that offense "occurs after the offender becomes a tier I sex offender." Thus, any sex offender whose registration offense is punishable by more than one year of imprisonment who has a prior sex offense conviction is at least in tier II. Likewise, section 111(4)(C) places in tier III any sex offender whose registration offense is punishable by imprisonment for more than one year, where that offense "occurs after the offender becomes a tier II sex offender." Thus, any sex offender whose registration offense is punishable by more than one year of imprisonment, and who at the time of that offense already satisfied the criteria for inclusion in tier II, is in tier III.

In determining tier enhancements based on recidivism, prior convictions must be taken into account regardless of when they occurred, including convictions occurring prior to the enactment of SORNA or its implementation in a particular jurisdiction. For example, consider an individual who was previously convicted for committing a sexual contact offense (punishable by more than a year of imprisonment) against a 13-year-old victim in 2000, and who is subsequently convicted for committing a sexual contact offense (punishable by more than a year of imprisonment) against a 14-year-old victim in 2010. While the later offense would not in itself support tier III classification on the basis of section 111(4)(A)(ii), since the victim was not below 13, tier III treatment would nevertheless be required on the ground of recidivism, since the earlier offense satisfied the criterion for tier II classification under section 111(3)(A)(iv). It may not always be possible, however, to obtain a complete record of an offender's prior convictions, particularly when they occurred many years or decades ago, and available criminal history information may be uninformative as to factors such as victim age that can affect the SORNA tier classification. Jurisdictions may rely on the methods and standards they normally use in searching criminal records and on the information appearing in the records so obtained in assessing SORNA tier enhancements based on recidivism.

In applying the SORNA tier definitions, it should be kept in mind that their significance under SORNA is in determining the extent of registration and notification requirements for offenders within the SORNA registration categories, and that they do not constitute independent requirements for jurisdictions to register offenders for whom SORNA does not otherwise require registration. In particular, the class of juvenile delinquents who are required to register under SORNA is defined by section 111(8), a class that is narrower in a number of respects than the class of offenders who satisfy the criteria for tier III classification under section 111(4). (See the discussion of section 111(8) in Part IV.A of these Guidelines above.) Hence, a juvenile delinquent's satisfaction of the criteria for tier III classification under section 111(4) does not in itself mean that a jurisdiction must require the juvenile to register in order to comply with

25

SORNA. Rather, that is only the case if the juvenile satisfies the criteria for required registration of juvenile delinquents under section 111(8).

VI.   REQUIRED REGISTRATION INFORMATION

Section 114 of SORNA defines the required minimum informational content of sex offender registries. It is divided into two lists. The first list, set forth in subsection (a) of section 114, describes information that the registrant will normally be in a position to provide. The second list, set forth in subsection (b), describes information that is likely to require some affirmative action by the jurisdiction to obtain, beyond asking the sex offender for the information. Supplementary to the information that the statute explicitly describes, section 114(a)(7) and (b)(8) authorize the Attorney General to specify additional information that must be obtained and included in the registry. This expansion authority is utilized to require including in the registries a number of additional types of information, such as information about registrants' e-mail addresses, telephone numbers, and the like, information concerning the whereabouts of registrants who lack fixed abodes or definite places of employment, and information about temporary lodging, as discussed below.

Whether a type of information must be obtained by a jurisdiction and included in its sex offender registry is a distinct question from whether the jurisdiction must make that information available to the public. Many of the informational items whose inclusion in the registry is required by section 114 and these Guidelines are not subject to a public disclosure requirement under SORNA, and some are exempt from public disclosure on a mandatory basis. The public disclosure requirements under SORNA and exceptions thereto are explained in Part VII of these Guidelines.

In order to implement requirements for the sharing of registration information appearing in other sections of SORNA (sections 113(c), 119(b), 121(b)—*see* Parts VII and X of these Guidelines for discussion), jurisdictions will need to maintain all required registration information in digitized form that will enable it to be immediately accessed by or transmitted to various entities. Hence, the jurisdiction's registry must be an electronic database, and descriptions of required types of information in section 114 should consistently be understood as referring to digitizable information rather than hard copies or physical objects. This does not mean, however, that all required registration information must be reproduced in a single segregated database, since the same effect may be achieved by including in the central registry database links or identification numbers that provide access to the information in other databases in which it is included (e.g., with respect to criminal history, fingerprint, and DNA information). These points are further discussed in connection with the relevant informational items.

As with SORNA's requirements generally, the informational requirements of section 114 and these Guidelines define a floor, not a ceiling, for jurisdictions' registries. Hence, jurisdictions are free to obtain and include in their registries a broader range of information than the minimum requirements described in this Part.

The required minimum informational content for sex offender registries is as follows:

- NAME, ALIASES, AND REMOTE COMMUNICATION IDENTIFIERS AND ADDRESSES (§ 114(a)(1), (a)(7)):

  ○ NAMES AND ALIASES (§ 114(a)(1)): The registry must include "[t]he name of the sex offender (including any alias used by the individual)." The names and aliases required by this provision include, in addition to registrants' primary or given names, nicknames and pseudonyms generally, regardless of the context in which they are used, any designations or monikers used for self-identification in Internet communications or postings, and ethnic or tribal names by which they are commonly known.

  ○ INTERNET IDENTIFIERS AND ADDRESSES (§ 114(a)(7)): In the context of Internet communications there may be no clear line between names or aliases that are required to be registered under SORNA § 114(a)(1) and addresses that are used for routing purposes. Moreover, regardless of the label, including in registries information on designations used by sex offenders for purposes of routing or self-identification in Internet communications—e.g., e-mail and instant messaging addresses—serves the underlying purposes of sex offender registration and notification. Among other potential uses, having this information may help in investigating crimes committed online by registered sex offenders—such as attempting to lure children or trafficking in child pornography through the Internet—and knowledge by sex offenders that their Internet identifiers are known to the authorities may help to discourage them from engaging in such criminal activities. The authority under section 114(a)(7) is accordingly exercised to require that the information included in the registries must include all designations used by sex offenders for purposes of routing or self-identification in Internet communications or postings.

  ○ TELEPHONE NUMBERS (§ 114(a)(7)): Requiring sex offenders to provide their telephone numbers (both for fixed location phones and cell phones) furthers the objectives of sex offender registration. One obvious purpose in having such information is to facilitate communication between registration personnel and a sex offender in case issues arise relating to the sex offender's registration. Moreover, as communications technology advances, the boundaries blur between text-based and voice-based communications media. Telephone calls may be transmitted through the Internet. Text messages may be sent between cell phones. Regardless of the particular communication medium, and regardless of whether the communication involves text or voice, sex offenders may potentially utilize remote communications in efforts to contact or lure potential victims. Hence, including phone numbers in the registration information may help in investigating crimes committed by registrants that involved telephonic communication with the victim, and knowledge that their phone numbers are known to the authorities may help sex offenders to resist the temptation to commit crimes by this means. The authority under section 114(a)(7) is accordingly exercised to require that the information included in the registries must include sex offenders' telephone numbers and any other designations used by sex offenders for purposes of routing or self-identification in telephonic communications.

- SOCIAL SECURITY NUMBER (§ 114(a)(2), (a)(7)): The registry must include "[t]he Social Security number of the sex offender." In addition to any valid Social Security number issued to the registrant by the government, the information the jurisdiction requires registrants to provide under this heading must include any number that the registrant uses as his or her purported Social Security number since registrants may, for example, attempt to use false Social Security numbers in seeking employment that would provide access to children. To the extent that purported (as opposed to actual) Social Security numbers may be beyond the scope of the information required by section 114(a)(2), the authority under section 114(a)(7) is exercised to require that information on such purported numbers be obtained and included in the registry as well.

- RESIDENCE, LODGING, AND TRAVEL INFORMATION (§ 114(a)(3), (a)(7)):

  - RESIDENCE ADDRESS (§ 114(a)(3)): The registry must include "the address of each residence at which the sex offender resides or will reside." As provided in SORNA § 111(13), residence refers to "the location of the individual's home or other place where the individual habitually lives." (For more as to the meaning of "resides" under SORNA, *see* Part VIII of these Guidelines.) The statute refers to places in which the sex offender "will reside" so as to cover situations in which, for example, a sex offender is initially being registered prior to release from imprisonment, and hence is not yet residing in the place or location to which he or she expects to go following release.

  - OTHER RESIDENCE INFORMATION (§ 114(a)(7)): Sex offenders who lack fixed abodes are nevertheless required to register in the jurisdictions in which they reside, as discussed in Part VIII of these Guidelines. Such sex offenders cannot provide the residence address required by section 114(a)(3) because they have no definite "address" at which they live. Nevertheless, some more or less specific description should normally be obtainable concerning the place or places where such a sex offender habitually lives—e.g., information about a certain part of a city that is the sex offender's habitual locale, a park or spot on the street (or a number of such places) where the sex offender stations himself during the day or sleeps at night, shelters among which the sex offender circulates, or places in public buildings, restaurants, libraries, or other establishments that the sex offender frequents. Having this type of location information serves the same public safety purposes as knowing the whereabouts of sex offenders with definite residence addresses. Hence, the authority under SORNA § 114(a)(7) is exercised to require that information be obtained about where sex offenders who lack fixed abodes habitually live with whatever definiteness is possible under the circumstances. Likewise, in relation to sex offenders who lack a residence address for any other reason—e.g., a sex offender who lives in a house in a rural or tribal area that has no street address—the registry must include information that

28

identifies where the individual has his or her home or habitually lives.

○ TEMPORARY LODGING INFORMATION (§ 114(a)(7)): Sex offenders who reoffend may commit new offenses at locations away from the places in which they have a permanent or long-term presence. Indeed, to the extent that information about sex offenders' places of residence is available to the authorities, but information is lacking concerning their temporary lodging elsewhere, the relative attractiveness to sex offenders of molesting children or committing other sexual crimes while traveling or visiting away from home increases. Hence, to achieve the objectives of sex offender registration, it is valuable to have information about other places in which sex offenders are staying, even if only temporarily. The authority under SORNA § 114(a)(7) is accordingly exercised to provide that jurisdictions must require sex offenders to provide information about any place in which the sex offender is staying when away from his residence for seven or more days, including identifying the place and the period of time the sex offender is staying there. The benefits of having this information include facilitating the successful investigation of crimes committed by sex offenders while away from their normal places of residence, employment, or school attendance, and decreasing the attractiveness to sex offenders of committing crimes in such circumstances.

○ TRAVEL AND IMMIGRATION DOCUMENTS (§ 114(a)(7)): The authority under SORNA § 114(a)(7) is exercised to provide that registrants must be required to produce or provide information about their passports, if they have passports, and that registrants who are aliens must be required to produce or provide information about documents establishing their immigration status. The registry must include digitized copies of these documents, document type and number information for such documents, or links to another database or databases that contain such information. Having this type of information in the registries serves various purposes, including helping to locate and apprehend registrants who may attempt to leave the United States after committing new sex offenses or registration violations; facilitating the tracking and identification of registrants who leave the United States but later reenter while still required to register (*see* SORNA § 128); and crosschecking the accuracy and completeness of other types of information that registrants are required to provide—e.g., if immigration documents show that an alien registrant is in the United States on a student visa but the registrant fails to provide information concerning the school attended as required by SORNA § 114(a)(5).

● EMPLOYMENT INFORMATION (§ 114(a)(4), (a)(7)):

○ EMPLOYER NAME AND ADDRESS (§ 114(a)(4)): The registry must include "[t]he name and address of any place where the sex offender is an employee or will be an employee." SORNA § 111(12) explains that "employee" includes "an individual who is self-employed or works for any other entity, whether

29

compensated or not." As the definitional provisions indicate, the information required under this heading is not limited to information relating to compensated work or a regular occupation, but includes as well name and address information for any place where the registrant works as a volunteer or otherwise works without remuneration. The statute refers to places in which the sex offender "will be an employee" so as to cover, for example, cases in which a sex offender is initially being registered prior to release from imprisonment and has secured employment that will commence upon his release, and other circumstances in which a sex offender reports an initiation or change of employment to a jurisdiction before the new employment commences. It does not mean that jurisdictions must include in their registries merely speculative information sex offenders have provided about places they may work in the future.

○ OTHER EMPLOYMENT INFORMATION (§ 114(a)(7)): A sex offender who is employed may not have a fixed place of employment—e.g., a long-haul trucker whose "workplace" is roads and highways throughout the country, a self-employed handyman who works out of his home and does repair or home-improvement work at other people's homes, or a person who frequents sites that contractors visit to obtain day labor and works for whatever contractor hires him on a given day. Knowing as far as possible where such a sex offender is in the course of employment serves the same public safety purposes as the corresponding information regarding a sex offender who is employed at a fixed location. The authority under section 114(a)(7) is accordingly exercised to require that information be obtained and included in the registry concerning the places where such a sex offender works with whatever definiteness is possible under the circumstances, such as information about normal travel routes or the general area(s) in which the sex offender works.

○ PROFESSIONAL LICENSES (§ 114(a)(7)): The authority under section 114(a)(7) is exercised to require that information be obtained and included in the registry concerning all licensing of the registrant that authorizes the registrant to engage in an occupation or carry out a trade or business. Information of this type may be helpful in locating the registrant if he or she absconds, may provide a basis for notifying the responsible licensing authority if the registrant's conviction of a sex offense may affect his or her eligibility for the license, and may be useful in crosschecking the accuracy and completeness of other information the registrant is required to provide—e.g., if the registrant is licensed to engage in a certain occupation but does not provide name or place of employment information as required by section 114(a)(4) for such an occupation.

● SCHOOL INFORMATION (§ 114(a)(5)): The registry must include "[t]he name and address of any place where the sex offender is a student or will be a student." Section 111(11) defines "student" to mean "an individual who enrolls in or attends an educational institution, including (whether public or private) a secondary school, trade or professional school, and institution of higher education." As the statutory definition indicates, the requirement extends to all types of educational institutions. Hence, this information must be provided for private schools as well as public schools, including both parochial and non-parochial private schools, and regardless of whether the educational institution is attended for purposes of secular, religious, or cultural studies. The registration information requirement of section 114(a)(5) refers to the names and addresses of educational institutions where a sex offender has or will have a physical presence as a student. It does not require information about a sex offender's participating in courses only remotely through the mail or the Internet. (Internet identifiers and addresses used by a sex offender in such remote communications, however, must be included in the registration information as provided in the discussion of "INTERNET IDENTIFIERS AND ADDRESSES" earlier in this list.) As with residence and employment information, the statute refers to information about places the sex offender "will be" a student so as to cover, for example, circumstances in which a sex offender reports to a jurisdiction that he has enrolled in a school prior to his commencement of attendance at that school. It does not mean that jurisdictions must include in their registries merely speculative information sex offenders have provided about places they may attend school in the future.

- VEHICLE INFORMATION (§ 114(a)(6), (a)(7)): The registry must include "[t]he license plate number and a description of any vehicle owned or operated by the sex offender." This includes, in addition to vehicles registered to the sex offender, any vehicle that the sex offender regularly drives, either for personal use or in the course of employment. A sex offender may not regularly use a particular vehicle or vehicles in the course of employment, but may have access to a large number of vehicles for employment purposes, such as using many vehicles from an employer's fleet in a delivery job. In a case of this type, jurisdictions are not required to obtain information concerning all such vehicles to satisfy SORNA's minimum informational requirements, but jurisdictions are free to require such information if they are so inclined. The authority under § 114(a)(7) is exercised to define and expand the required information concerning vehicles in two additional respects. First, the term "vehicle" should be understood to include watercraft and aircraft, in addition to land vehicles, so descriptive information must be required for all such vehicles owned or operated by the sex offender. The information must include the license plate number if it is a type of vehicle for which license plates are issued, or if it has no license plate but does have some other type of registration number or identifier, then information concerning such a registration number or identifier must be included. To the extent that any of the information described above may be beyond the scope of section 114(a)(6), the authority under section 114(a)(7) is exercised to provide that it must be obtained and included in the registry. Second, the sex offender must be required to provide and the registry must include information concerning the place or places where the registrant's vehicle or vehicles are habitually parked, docked, or otherwise kept. Having information of this type may help to prevent flight, facilitate investigation, or effect an apprehension if the registrant is implicated in the commission of new offenses or violates registration requirements.

- DATE OF BIRTH (§ 114(a)(7)). The authority under § 114(a)(7) is exercised to require date of birth information for registrants, which must be included in the registry. Since date of birth is regularly utilized as part of an individual's basic identification information, having this information in the registry is of obvious value in helping to identify, track, and locate registrants. The information the jurisdiction requires registrants to provide under this heading must include any date that the registrant uses as his or her purported date of birth—not just his or her actual date of birth—since registrants may, for example, provide false date of birth information in seeking employment that would provide access to children.

- PHYSICAL DESCRIPTION (§ 114(b)(1)): The registry must include "[a] physical description of the sex offender." This must include a description of the general physical appearance or characteristics of the sex offender, and any identifying marks, such as scars or tattoos.

- TEXT OF REGISTRATION OFFENSE (§ 114(b)(2)): The registry must include "[t]he text of the provision of law defining a criminal offense for which the sex offender is registered." As with other information in the registries, this does not mean that the registry must be a paper records system that includes a hard copy of the statute defining the registration offense. Rather, the registry must be an electronic database, and the relevant statutory provision must be included as electronic text. Alternatively, this requirement can be satisfied by including in the central registry database a link or citation to the statute defining the registration offense if: (i) doing so provides online access to the linked or cited provision, and (ii) the link or citation will continue to provide access to the offense as formulated at the time the registrant was convicted of it, even if the defining statute is subsequently amended.

- CRIMINAL HISTORY AND OTHER CRIMINAL JUSTICE INFORMATION (§ 114(b)(3)): The registry must include "[t]he criminal history of the sex offender, including the date of all arrests and convictions; the status of parole, probation, or supervised release; registration status [i.e., whether the sex offender is in violation of the registration requirement and unlocatable]; and the existence of any outstanding arrest warrants for the sex offender." This requirement can be satisfied by including the specified types of information in the central registry database, or by including in that database links or identifying numbers that provide access to these types of information in criminal justice databases that contain them.

- CURRENT PHOTOGRAPH (§ 114(b)(4)): The registry information must include "[a] current photograph of the sex offender." As with other information in the registries, this does not mean that the registry must be a paper records system that includes physical photographs. Rather, the photographs of sex offenders must be included in digitized form in an electronic registry, so as to permit the electronic transmission of registration information that is necessary to implement other SORNA requirements. (For more about the taking of photographs and keeping them current, see the discussion of periodic in-person appearances in Part XI of these Guidelines.)

- FINGERPRINTS AND PALM PRINTS (§ 114(b)(5)): The registry information must include "[a] set of fingerprints and palm prints of the sex offender." As with other registration information, this should be understood to refer to digitized fingerprint and palm print information rather than physical fingerprint cards and palm prints. The requirement can be satisfied by including such digitized fingerprint and palm print information in the central registry database, or by providing links or identifying numbers in the central registry database that provide access to fingerprint and palm print information in other databases for each registered sex offender.

- DNA (§ 114(b)(6)): The registry information must include "[a] DNA sample of the sex offender." This means that a DNA sample must be taken, or must have been taken, from the sex offender, for purposes of analysis and entry of the resulting DNA profile into the Combined DNA Index System (CODIS). The requirement is satisfied by including information in the central registry database that confirms collection of such a sample from the sex offender for purposes of analysis and entry of the DNA profile into CODIS or inclusion of the sex offender's DNA profile in CODIS.

- DRIVER'S LICENSE OR IDENTIFICATION CARD (§ 114(b)(7)): The registry information must include "[a] photocopy of a valid driver's license or identification card issued to the sex offender by a jurisdiction." The requirement can be satisfied by including a digitized photocopy of the specified documents in the central registry database for each sex offender to whom such a document has been issued. Alternatively, it can be satisfied by including in the central registry database links or identifying numbers that provide access in other databases (such as a Department of Motor Vehicles database) to the information that would be shown by such a photocopy. As noted, this requirement pertains to sex offenders to whom drivers' licenses or identification cards have been issued. It does not mean that jurisdictions must issue drivers' licenses or identification cards to sex offenders to whom they would not otherwise issue such documents in order to create this type of information for inclusion in the registry.

VII. DISCLOSURE AND SHARING OF INFORMATION

The SORNA requirements for disclosure and sharing of information about registrants appear primarily in section 118, which is concerned with sex offender websites, and section 121, which is concerned with community notification in a broader sense and with some more targeted types of disclosures. The two sections will be discussed separately.

A. Sex Offender Websites

Section 118(a) of SORNA states a general rule that jurisdictions are to "make available on the Internet, in a manner that is readily accessible to all jurisdictions and to the public, all information about each sex offender in the registry." This general requirement is subject to certain mandatory and discretionary exemptions, appearing in subsections (b) and (c) of section 118, which are discussed below. As the later discussion explains, after the mandatory and discretionary exemptions are taken into account, the affirmative website posting requirements are limited to specified information concerning sex offenders' names, addresses or locations, vehicle descriptions and license plate numbers, physical descriptions, sex offenses for which convicted, and current photographs.

Currently, all 50 states, the District of Columbia, Puerto Rico, and Guam have sex offender websites that make information about registered sex offenders available to the public. The listed jurisdictions may need to modify their existing websites to varying degrees to implement the requirements of section 118.

Beyond stating a general rule of website posting for sex offender information (subject to exceptions and limitations as discussed below), subsection (a) of section 118 includes requirements about the field-search capabilities of the jurisdictions' websites. In part, it states that these field search capabilities must include searches by "zip code or geographic radius set by the user." In other words, the websites must be so designed that members of the public who access a website are able to specify particular zip code areas, and are able to specify geographic radii—e.g., within one mile of a specified address—and thereby bring up on the website the information about all of the posted sex offenders in the specified zip code or geographic area.

Subsection (a) of section 118 further states that each website "shall also include . . . all field search capabilities needed for full participation in the Dru Sjodin National Sex Offender Public Website and shall participate in that website as provided by the Attorney General." The statutory basis for the referenced National Sex Offender Public Website (NSOPW) appears in SORNA § 120. It is operated by the Department of Justice at the address www.nsopr.gov. All 50 states, the District of Columbia, Puerto Rico, and Guam currently participate in the NSOPW, which provides public access to the information in their respective sex offender websites through single-query searches on a national site. As noted, participation in the NSOPW is a required element of SORNA implementation. To satisfy the requirement under section 118(a) of having "all field search capabilities needed for full participation in the [NSOPW]," jurisdictions' sex offender websites must allow searches by name, county, and city/town, as well as having the zip code and geographic radius search capacities mentioned specifically in the statute.

Other SORNA requirements relating to sex offender websites are discussed in the remainder of this Subpart under the following headings: mandatory exemptions, discretionary exemptions and required inclusions, remote communication addresses, and other provisions.

MANDATORY EXEMPTIONS

Section 118(b)(1)-(3) identifies three types of information that are mandatorily exempt from disclosure, and section 118(b)(4) gives the Attorney General the authority to create additional mandatory exemptions. The limitations of subsection (b) only constrain jurisdictions in relation to the information made available on their publicly accessible sex offender websites. They do not limit the discretion of jurisdictions to disclose these types of information in other contexts. The types of information that are within the mandatory exemptions from public sex offender website disclosure are as follows:

- VICTIM IDENTITY: Section 118(b)(1) exempts "the identity of any victim of a sex offense." The purpose of this exemption is to protect victim privacy. So long as the victim is not identified, this does not limit jurisdictions' discretion to include on the website information about the nature and circumstances of the offense, which may include information relating to the victim, such as the age and gender of the victim, and the conduct engaged in by the sex offender against the victim.

- SOCIAL SECURITY NUMBER: Section 118(b)(2) exempts "the Social Security number of the sex offender."

- ARRESTS NOT RESULTING IN CONVICTION: Section 118(b)(3) exempts "any reference to arrests of the sex offender that did not result in conviction." As noted, this mandatory exemption, like the others, only affects the information that may be posted on a jurisdiction's public sex offender website. It does not limit a jurisdiction's use or disclosure of arrest information in any other context, such as disclosure to law enforcement agencies for law enforcement purposes, or disclosure to the public (by means other than posting on the sex offender website) under "open records" laws.

- TRAVEL AND IMMIGRATION DOCUMENT NUMBERS: The authority under section 118(b)(4) is exercised to exempt the numbers assigned to registrants' passports and immigration documents. This exemption reflects concerns that public posting of such information could facilitate identity theft and could provide a source of passport and immigration document numbers to individuals seeking to enter, remain in, or travel from the United States using forged documents or false identities. Like the other mandatory exemptions, this exemption only affects the information that may be posted on a jurisdiction's public sex offender website. It does not limit a jurisdiction's use or disclosure of registrants' travel or immigration document information in any other context, such as disclosure to agencies with law enforcement, immigration, or national security functions.

DISCRETIONARY EXEMPTIONS AND REQUIRED INCLUSIONS

Section 118(c)(1)-(3) provides three optional exemptions, which describe information that jurisdictions may exempt from their websites in their discretion. The first of these is "any information about a tier I sex offender convicted of an offense other than a specified offense against a minor." The meaning of "tier I sex offender" is explained in Part V of these Guidelines, and the meaning of "specified offense against a minor" is explained in Part IV.D of these Guidelines. The second and third optional exemptions are, respectively, "the name of an employer of the sex offender" and "the name of an educational institution where the sex offender is a student." As noted, these exclusions are discretionary. Jurisdictions are free to include these types of information on their sex offender websites if they are so inclined.

Section 118(c)(4) provides a further optional exemption of "any other information exempted from disclosure by the Attorney General." This authorization recognizes that there are some additional types of information that are required to be included in sex offender registries by section 114, but whose required disclosure through public sex offender websites may reasonably be regarded by particular jurisdictions as inappropriate or unnecessary. For example, public access to registrants' remote communication routing addresses (such as e-mail addresses) presents both risks and benefits. Minimizing the risks and maximizing the benefits depends on the appropriate design of the means and form of access. The recommended treatment of such information is discussed later in this Subpart. A number of other types of required registration information, such as fingerprints, palm prints, and DNA information, are primarily or exclusively of interest to law enforcement.

In positive terms, as set out in the list below, there are eight core types of information whose public disclosure through the sex offender websites has the greatest value in promoting public safety by enabling members of the public to identify sex offenders, to know where they are, and to know what crimes they have committed. The list below is an exhaustive list of the types of registration information that jurisdictions must include on their public sex offender websites to satisfy the requirements for SORNA implementation. All other types of registration information are excluded from required website posting, either on a mandatory basis under section 118(b), on a discretionary basis under section 118(c)(1)-(3), or on the basis of the Attorney General's authority to allow additional discretionary exemptions under section 118(c)(4). The list of informational items that jurisdictions must include on their public sex offender websites is as follows:

- The name of the sex offender, including any aliases.

- The address of each residence at which the sex offender resides or will reside and, if the sex offender does not have any (present or expected) residence address, other information about where the sex offender has his or her home or habitually lives. If current information of this type is not available because the sex offender is in violation of the requirement to register or unlocatable, the website must so note.

- The address of any place where the sex offender is an employee or will be an employee and, if the sex offender is employed but does not have a definite employment address, other information about where the sex offender works.

- The address of any place where the sex offender is a student or will be a student.

- The license plate number and a description of any vehicle owned or operated by the sex offender.

- A physical description of the sex offender.

- The sex offense for which the sex offender is registered and any other sex offense for which the sex offender has been convicted.

- A current photograph of the sex offender.

The foregoing list remains subject to the discretionary authority of jurisdictions under

36

section 118(c)(1) to exempt information about a tier I sex offender convicted of an offense other than a specified offense against a minor.

REMOTE COMMUNICATION ADDRESSES

Public access to or disclosure of sex offenders' remote communication routing addresses and their equivalent—such as e-mail addresses and telephone numbers—is discussed separately because the issue presents both risks and benefits and merits careful handling by jurisdictions.

On the one hand, appropriately designed forms of access to such information may further the public safety objectives of sex offender registration and notification. For example, the operators of Internet social networking services that serve children may validly wish to check whether the e-mail addresses of individuals on their user lists are those of registered sex offenders, so that they can prevent sex offenders from using their services as avenues for Internet luring of children for purposes of sexual abuse. Likewise, a parent may legitimately wish to check whether the e-mail address of an unknown individual who is communicating with his or her child over the Internet is that of a registered sex offender, for the same protective purpose.

On the other hand, some forms of public disclosure of this type of information—such as including sex offenders' e-mail addresses as part of the information in their individual listings on the sex offender websites, which also include their names, locations, etc.—could raise serious concerns about unintended consequences and misuse. Posting of the information in this form could provide ready access by sex offenders to the e-mail addresses of other sex offenders, thereby facilitating networking among such offenders through the Internet for such purposes as: exchanging information about or providing access to child victims for purposes of sexual abuse; recruiting confederates and accomplices for the purpose of committing child sexual abuse or exploitation offenses or other sexually violent crimes; trafficking in child pornography; and sharing ideas and information about how to commit sexual crimes, avoid detection and apprehension for committing such crimes, or evade registration requirements.

The public safety benefits of public access in this context may be realized, and the risks and concerns addressed, by not including remote communication routing addresses or information that would enable sex offenders to contact each other on the individual public website postings of registrants, but including on the websites a function by which members of the public may enter, e.g., an e-mail address or phone number and receive an answer whether the specified address or number has been registered as that of a sex offender. In the case of a concerned parent as described above, for example, this could enable the parent to ascertain that the e-mail address of an individual attempting to communicate through the Internet with his or her child is the address of a sex offender, but without providing sex offenders access to listings showing the e-mail addresses of other persons who may share their dispositions to commit sexual crimes.

Jurisdictions are accordingly permitted and encouraged to provide public access to remote communication address information included in the sex offender registries, in the form described above, i.e., a function that allows checking whether specified addresses are included in the registries as the addresses of sex offenders. The registry management and website software that the Justice Department is developing pursuant to SORNA § 123 will include software for such a website function.

OTHER PROVISIONS

The final three subsections in section 118 contain additional website specifications as follows:

Subsection (d) requires that sites "include, to the extent practicable, links to sex offender safety and education resources."

Subsection (e) requires that sites "include instructions on how to seek correction of information that an individual contends is erroneous." A jurisdiction could comply with this requirement, for example, by including on its website information identifying the jurisdiction's agency responsible for correcting erroneous information, and advising persons that they can contact this agency if they believe that information on the site is erroneous.

Subsection (f) requires that sites include "a warning that information on the site should not be used to unlawfully injure, harass, or commit a crime against any individual named in the registry or residing or working at any reported address," and further provides that the warning "shall note that any such action could result in civil or criminal penalties."

B. Community Notification and Targeted Disclosures

Section 121(b) of SORNA states that "immediately after a sex offender registers or updates a registration . . . the information in the registry (other than information exempted from disclosure by the Attorney General) about that offender" must be provided to various specified entities and individuals. The requirement that the information must be provided to the specified recipients "immediately" should be understood to mean that it must be provided within three business days. *Cf.* SORNA §§ 113(b)(2), 117(a) (equating within three business days and "immediately" in relation to initial registration). The requirement that the information be provided immediately is qualified by section 121(c), which provides that recipients described in section 121(b)(6)-(7)—i.e., volunteer organizations in which contact with minors or other vulnerable individuals might occur, and any organization, company, or individual who requests notification—"may opt to receive the notification . . . no less frequently than once every five business days."

These requirements will be discussed in turn in relation to two groups of recipients—a group of four types of recipients that require special treatment, followed by suggestions for a uniform approach in relation to the remaining types of recipients. The four types that require special treatment are as follows:

- NATIONAL DATABASES: Section 121(b)(1) states that the information is to be provided to "[t]he Attorney General, who shall include that information in the National

Sex Offender Registry or other appropriate databases." The National Sex Offender Registry (NSOR) is a national database maintained by the Federal Bureau of Investigation (FBI), which compiles information from the registration jurisdictions' sex offender registries and makes it available to criminal justice agencies on a nationwide basis. The current statutory basis for NSOR appears in SORNA § 119(a). The statute refers to the Attorney General including the information submitted by jurisdictions in NSOR "or other appropriate databases" because some types of registry information described in SORNA § 114, such as criminal history information, may be maintained by the FBI in other databases rather than directly in the NSOR database. In addition, the United States Marshals Service, which is the lead federal agency in investigating registration violations by sex offenders and assisting jurisdictions in enforcing their registration requirements, may establish an additional national database or databases to help in detecting, investigating, and apprehending sex offenders who violate registration requirements. Jurisdictions accordingly can implement the requirement of section 121(b)(1) by submitting to the FBI within three business days the types of registry information that the FBI includes in NSOR or other national databases, and by submitting information within the same time frame to other federal agencies (such as the United States Marshals Service) in conformity with any requirements the Department of Justice or the Marshals Service may adopt for this purpose.

- LAW ENFORCEMENT AND SUPERVISION AGENCIES: Section 121(b)(2), in part, identifies as further required recipients "[a]ppropriate law enforcement agencies (including probation agencies, if appropriate) . . . in each area in which the individual resides, is an employee or is a student." "Law enforcement agencies" should be understood to refer to agencies with criminal investigation or prosecution functions, such as police departments, sheriffs' offices, and district attorneys' offices. "Probation agencies, if appropriate" should be understood to refer to all offender supervision agencies that are responsible for a sex offender's supervision. Jurisdictions can implement the requirement of section 121(b)(2) by making registration information available to these agencies within three business days, by any effective means—permissible options include electronic transmission of registration information and provision of online access to registration information. Jurisdictions may define the relevant "area[s]" in which a registrant resides, is an employee, or is a student for purposes of section 121(b)(2) in accordance with their own policies, or may avoid the need to have to specify such areas by providing access to sex offender registry information to law enforcement and supervision agencies generally, since doing so makes the information available to recipients in all areas (however defined). The authority under the introductory language in section 121(b) to exempt information from disclosure is not exercised in relation to these recipients with respect to any of the information required to be included in registries under section 114 because law enforcement and supervision agencies need access to complete information about sex offenders to carry out their protective, investigative, prosecutorial, and supervisory functions.

- JURISDICTIONS: Section 121(b)(3) identifies as required recipients "[e]ach jurisdiction where the sex offender resides, is an employee, or is a student, and each jurisdiction from or to which a change of residence, employment, or student status occurs." This is part of a broader group of SORNA provisions concerning the exchange of registration information among jurisdictions and ensuring that all relevant jurisdictions have such information in an up-to-date form. The implementation of section 121(b)(3) and other provisions relating to these matters is discussed in Parts IX and X of these Guidelines.

- NATIONAL CHILD PROTECTION ACT AGENCIES: Section 121(b)(4) identifies as required recipients "[a]ny agency responsible for conducting employment-related background checks under section 3 of the National Child Protection Act of 1993 (42 U.S.C. 5119a)." The National Child Protection Act (NCPA) provides procedures under which qualified entities (e.g., prospective employers of child care providers) may request an authorized state agency to conduct a criminal history background check to obtain information bearing on an individual's fitness to have responsibility for the safety and well-being of children, the elderly, or individuals with disabilities. The authorized agency makes a determination whether the individual who is the subject of the background check has been convicted of, or is under indictment for, a crime bearing on the individual's fitness for such responsibilities, and conveys that determination to the qualified entity. Considering the nature of the recipients under section 121(b)(4) and the functions for which they need information about sex offenders, jurisdictions can implement section 121(b)(4) by making available to such agencies (i.e., those authorized to conduct NCPA background checks) within three business days all criminal history information in the registry relevant to the conduct of such background checks.

Beyond the four categories specified above, section 121(b) requires that sex offender registration information be provided to several other types of recipients, as follows:

- Each school and public housing agency in each area in which the sex offender resides, is an employee, or is a student (section 121(b)(2)).

- Social service entities responsible for protecting minors in the child welfare system (section 121(b)(5)).

- Volunteer organizations in which contact with minors or other vulnerable individuals might occur (section 121(b)(6)).

- Any organization, company, or individual who requests such notification pursuant to procedures established by the jurisdiction (section 121(b)(7)).

Implementing the required provision of information about registrants to these entities potentially presents a number of difficulties for jurisdictions, such as problems in identifying and maintaining comprehensive lists of recipients in these categories, keeping those lists up to date, subdividing recipients by "area" with respect to the notification under section 121(b)(2), and developing means of transmitting or providing access to the information for the various types of recipients. The objectives of these provisions, however, can be achieved by augmenting public sex offender websites to include appropriate notification functions. Specifically, a jurisdiction will be deemed to have satisfied the requirements of these provisions of section 121(b) if it adopts an automated notification system that incorporates substantially the following features:

- The information required to be included on sex offender websites, as described in Part VII.A of these Guidelines, is posted on the jurisdiction's sex offender website within three business days.

- The jurisdiction's sex offender website includes a function under which members of the public and organizations can request notification when sex offenders commence residence, employment, or school attendance within zip code or geographic radius areas specified by the requester, where the requester provides an e-mail address to which the notice is to be sent.

- Upon posting on the jurisdiction's sex offender website of new residence, employment, or school attendance information for a sex offender within an area specified by the requester, the system automatically sends an e-mail notice to the requester that identifies the sex offender, thus enabling the requester to access the jurisdiction's website and view the new information about the sex offender.

VIII. WHERE REGISTRATION IS REQUIRED

Section 113(a) of SORNA provides that a sex offender shall register and keep the registration current in each jurisdiction in which the sex offender resides, is an employee, or is a student. Section 113(a) of SORNA further provides that, for initial registration purposes only, a sex offender must also register in the jurisdiction in which convicted if it is different from the jurisdiction of residence.

Starting with the last-mentioned requirement—registration in jurisdiction of conviction if different from jurisdiction of residence—in some cases the jurisdiction in which a sex offender is convicted is not the same as the jurisdiction to which the sex offender goes to live immediately following release. For example, a resident of jurisdiction A is convicted for a sex offense in jurisdiction B. After being released following imprisonment or sentenced to probation in jurisdiction B, the sex offender returns immediately to jurisdiction A. Although jurisdiction B is not the sex offender's jurisdiction of residence following his release or sentencing, jurisdiction B as the convicting jurisdiction is in the best position initially to take registration information from the sex offender and to inform him of his registration obligations, as required by SORNA § 117(a), and is likely to be the only jurisdiction in a position to do so within the time frames specified in SORNA §§ 113(b) and 117(a)—i.e., before release from imprisonment, or within 3 business days of sentencing for a sex offender with a non-incarcerative sentence. Hence, SORNA § 113(a) provides for initial registration in the jurisdiction of conviction in such cases. SORNA, however, never requires continued registration in the jurisdiction of conviction if the sex offender does not reside, work, or attend school in that jurisdiction.

Beyond the special case of initial registration in the conviction jurisdiction where it differs from the residence jurisdiction, section 113(a) requires both registration and keeping the registration current in each jurisdiction where a sex offender resides, is an employee, or is a student. Starting with jurisdictions of residence, this means that a sex offender must initially register in the jurisdiction of residence if it is the jurisdiction of conviction, and must thereafter register in any other jurisdiction in which the sex offender subsequently resides.

The notion of "residence" requires definition for this purpose. Requiring registration only where a sex offender has a residence or home in the sense of a fixed abode would be too narrow to achieve SORNA's objective of "comprehensive" registration of sex offenders (*see* § 102), because some sex offenders have no fixed abodes. For example, a sex offender may be homeless, living on the street or moving from shelter to shelter, or a sex offender may live in something that itself moves from place to place, such as a mobile home, trailer, or houseboat. SORNA § 111(13) accordingly defines "resides" to mean "the location of the individual's home or other place where the individual habitually lives." This entails that a sex offender must register:

- in any jurisdiction in which he has his home; and

- in any jurisdiction in which he habitually lives (even if he has no home or fixed address in the jurisdiction, or no home anywhere).

The scope of "habitually lives" in this context is not self-explanatory and requires further definition. An overly narrow definition would undermine the objectives of sex offender registration and notification under SORNA. For example, consider the case of a sex offender who nominally has his home in one jurisdiction—e.g., he maintains a mail drop there, or identifies his place of residence for legal purposes as his parents' home, where he visits occasionally—but he lives most of the time with his girlfriend in an adjacent jurisdiction. Registration in the nominal home jurisdiction alone in such a case would mean that the registration information is not informative as to where the sex offender is actually residing, and hence would not fulfill the public safety objectives of tracking sex offenders' whereabouts following their release into the community.

"Habitually lives" accordingly should be understood to include places in which the sex offender lives with some regularity, and with reference to where the sex offender actually lives, not just in terms of what he would choose to characterize as his home address or place of residence for self-interested reasons. The specific interpretation of this element of "residence" these Guidelines adopt is that a sex offender habitually lives in the relevant sense in any place in which the sex offender lives for at least 30 days. Hence, a sex offender resides in a jurisdiction for purposes of SORNA if the sex offender has a home in the jurisdiction, or if the sex offender lives in the jurisdiction for at least 30 days. Jurisdictions may specify in the manner of their choosing the application of the 30-day standard to sex offenders whose presence in the jurisdiction is intermittent but who live in the jurisdiction for 30 days in the aggregate over some longer period of time. Like other aspects of SORNA, the requirement to register sex offenders who "reside" in the jurisdiction as defined in section 111(13) is a minimum requirement, and jurisdictions in their discretion may require registration more broadly (for example, based on presence in the jurisdiction for a period shorter than 30 days).

As to the timing of registration based on changes of residence, the understanding of "habitually lives" to mean living in a place for at least 30 days does not mean that the registration of a sex offender who enters a jurisdiction to reside may be delayed until after he has lived in the jurisdiction for 30 days. Rather, a sex offender who enters a jurisdiction in order to make his home or habitually live in the jurisdiction must be required to register within three business days, as discussed in Part X.A of these Guidelines. Likewise, a sex offender who changes his place of residence within a jurisdiction must be required to report the change within three business days, as discussed in Part X.A.

SORNA also requires sex offenders to register and keep the registration current in any jurisdiction in which the sex offender is an employee. Hence, a sex offender who resides in jurisdiction A and commutes to work in an adjacent jurisdiction B must register and keep the registration current in both jurisdictions—in jurisdiction A as a resident, and in jurisdiction B as an employee. SORNA § 111(12) defines "employee" for this purpose to include "an individual who is self-employed or works for any other entity, whether compensated or not." As with residence, the SORNA requirement to register in jurisdictions of employment is not limited to sex offenders who have fixed places of employment or definite employment addresses. For example, consider a person residing in jurisdiction A who works out of his home as a handyman, regularly doing repair or home-improvement work at other people's houses both in jurisdiction A and in an adjacent jurisdiction B. Since the sex offender works in both jurisdictions, he must register in jurisdiction B as well as jurisdiction A.

The implementation measure for these SORNA requirements is for jurisdictions to require sex offenders who are employed in the jurisdiction, as described above, to register in the jurisdiction. If a sex offender has some employment-related presence in a jurisdiction, but does not have a fixed place of employment or regularly work within the jurisdiction, line drawing questions may arise, and jurisdictions may resolve these questions based on their own judgments. For example, if a sex offender who is a long haul trucker regularly drives through dozens of jurisdictions in the course of his employment, it is not required that all such jurisdictions must make the sex offender register based on his transient employment-related presence, but rather they may treat such cases in accordance with their own policies. (For more about required employment information, see the discussion in Part VI of these Guidelines.)

The final SORNA basis of registration is being a student, which SORNA § 111(11) defines to mean "an individual who enrolls in or attends an educational institution, including (whether public or private) a secondary school, trade or professional school, and institution of higher education." Hence, for example, a sex offender who resides in jurisdiction A, and is enrolled in a college in an adjacent jurisdiction B to which he commutes for classes, must be required to register in jurisdiction B as well as jurisdiction A. School enrollment or attendance in this context should be understood as referring to attendance at a school in a physical sense. It does not mean that a jurisdiction has to require a sex offender in some distant jurisdiction to register in the jurisdiction based on his taking a correspondence course through the mail with a school in the jurisdiction, or based on his taking courses at the school remotely through the Internet, unless the participation in the educational program also involves some physical attendance at the school in the jurisdiction.

In the context of SORNA's requirements concerning the jurisdictions in which sex offenders must register, as in all other contexts under SORNA and these Guidelines, "jurisdiction" has the meaning given in SORNA § 111(10)—i.e., it refers to the 50 States, the District of Columbia, the five principal territories, and Indian tribes so qualifying under section 127. Hence, for example, if a sex offender resides in one county in a state but works in a different county in the same state, the state may wish to require the sex offender to appear for registration purposes before the responsible officials in both counties. But this is not a matter that SORNA addresses. Rather, the relevant "jurisdiction" for SORNA purposes in such a case is simply the state, and finer questions about particular locations, political subdivisions, or areas within the state in which a sex offender will be required to register are matters of state discretion under SORNA.

IX.   INITIAL REGISTRATION

Under sections 113(b) and 117(a) of SORNA, jurisdictions must normally require that sex offenders be initially registered before release from imprisonment for the registration offense or, in case of a non-imprisonment sentence, within three business days of sentencing for the registration offense. Upon entry of the registration information into the registry, the initial registration jurisdiction must immediately forward the registration information to all other jurisdictions in which the sex offender is required to register. This is required by SORNA § 121(b)(3) (registration information is to be provided immediately to "[e]ach jurisdiction where the sex offender resides, is an employee, or is a student."). Hence, for example, if an imprisoned sex offender advises the conviction jurisdiction on initial registration that he will be residing in another jurisdiction following release, or that he will stay in the conviction jurisdiction but will be commuting to work in another jurisdiction, the conviction jurisdiction must notify the expected residence or employment jurisdiction by forwarding to that jurisdiction the sex offender's registration information (including the information about the expected residence or employment in that jurisdiction). The sex offender will then be required to make an in-person registration appearance within three business days of commencing residence or employment in that jurisdiction, as discussed in Part X of these Guidelines.

With respect to sex offenders released from imprisonment, section 117(a) states that the initial registration procedures are to be carried out "shortly before release of the sex offender from custody." "Shortly" does not prescribe a specific time frame, but jurisdictions should implement this requirement in light of the underlying objectives of ensuring that sex offenders have their registration obligations in mind when they are released, and avoiding situations in which registration information changes significantly between the time the initial registration procedures are carried out and the time the offender is released. However, jurisdictions are also encouraged, as a matter of sound policy, to effect initial registration with sufficient time in advance whenever possible so that the following can be done before the sex offender is released into the community: (i) subjecting the registration information provided by the sex offender to any verification the jurisdiction carries out to ensure accuracy (e.g., cross checking with other records), (ii) obtaining any information needed for the registry that must be secured from sources other than the sex offender, (iii) posting of the sex offender's information on the jurisdiction's sex offender website, and (iv) effecting other required notifications and disclosures of information relating to the sex offender.

The specific initial registration procedures required by section 117(a) are as follows:

- Informing the sex offender of his or her duties under SORNA and explaining those duties. (Of course if the jurisdiction adopts registration requirements that encompass but go beyond the SORNA minimum, the sex offender should be informed of the full range of duties, not only those required by SORNA.)

- Requiring the sex offender to read and sign a form stating that the duty to register has been explained and that the sex offender understands the registration requirement.

- Ensuring that the sex offender is registered—i.e., obtaining the required registration information for the sex offender and submitting that information for inclusion in the registry.

SORNA §§ 113(d) and 117(b) recognize that the normal initial registration procedure described above will not be feasible in relation to certain special classes of sex offenders, and provides that the Attorney General may prescribe alternative rules for the registration of such sex offenders. The specific problem is one of timing; it is not always possible to carry out the initial registration procedures for sex offenders who are required to register under SORNA prior to release from imprisonment (or within three days of sentencing) for the registration offense. The situations in which there may be problems of this type, and the rules adopted for those situations, are as follows:

RETROACTIVE CLASSES

As discussed in Part II.C of these Guidelines, SORNA applies to all sex offenders, including those convicted of their registration offenses prior to the enactment of SORNA or prior to particular jurisdictions' incorporation of the SORNA requirements into their programs. Jurisdictions are specifically required to register such sex offenders if they remain in the system as prisoners, supervisees, or registrants, or if they later reenter the system because of conviction for some other crime (whether or not the new crime is a sex offense).

In some cases this will create no difficulty for registering these sex offenders in conformity with the normal SORNA registration procedures. For example, suppose that a sex offender is convicted of an offense in the SORNA registration categories in 2005, that the jurisdiction implements SORNA in its registration program in 2008, and that the sex offender is released on completion of imprisonment in 2010. Such a sex offender can be registered prior to release from imprisonment in the same manner as sex offenders convicted following the enactment of SORNA and its implementation by the jurisdiction.

But in other cases this will not be possible, as illustrated by the following examples:

- *Example 1:* A sex offender convicted by a state for an offense in the SORNA registration categories is sentenced to probation, or released on post-imprisonment supervision, in 2005. The sex offender is not registered near the time of sentencing or before release from imprisonment, because the state did not require registration for the offense in question at that time. The state subsequently implements SORNA in 2008, which will include registering such a sex offender. But it is impossible to do so near the time of his sentencing or before his release from imprisonment, because that time is past. Likewise, a person convicted of a sex offense by an Indian tribal court in, e.g., 2005 may have not been registered near the time of sentencing or release because the tribe had not yet established any sex offender registration program at the time. If the person remains under supervision when the tribe implements SORNA, registration will be required by the SORNA standards, but the normal time frame for initial registration under SORNA will have passed some years ago, so registration within that time frame is impossible.

- *Example 2*: A sex offender is required to register for life by a jurisdiction based on a rape conviction in 1995 for which he was released from imprisonment in 2005. The sex offender was initially registered prior to his release from imprisonment on the basis of the jurisdiction's existing law, but the information concerning registration duties he was given at the time of release did not include telling him that he would have to appear periodically in person to verify and update the registration information (as required by SORNA § 116), because the jurisdiction did not have such a requirement at the time. So the sex offender will have to be required to appear periodically for verification and will have to be given new instructions about that as part of the jurisdiction's implementation of SORNA.

- *Example 3*: A sex offender convicted in 1980 for an offense subject to lifetime registration under SORNA is released from imprisonment in 1990 but is not required to register at the time because the jurisdiction had not yet established a sex offender registration program. In 2010, following the jurisdiction's implementation of SORNA, the sex offender reenters the system because of conviction for a robbery. The jurisdiction will need to require the sex offender to register based on his 1980 conviction for a sex offense when he is released from imprisonment for the robbery offense. But it is not possible to carry out the initial registration procedure for the sex offender prior to his release from imprisonment for the registration offense—i.e., the sex offense for which he was convicted in 1980—because that time is past.

With respect to sex offenders with pre-SORNA or pre-SORNA-implementation convictions who remain in the prisoner, supervision, or registered sex offender populations at the time of implementation—illustrated by the examples in the first and second bullets above—jurisdictions should endeavor to register them in conformity with SORNA as quickly as possible, including fully instructing them about the SORNA requirements, obtaining signed acknowledgments of such instructions, and obtaining and entering into the registry all information about them required under SORNA. But this may entail newly registering or re-registering a large number of sex offenders in the existing sex offender population, and it may not be feasible for a jurisdiction to do so immediately. Jurisdictions are accordingly authorized to phase in SORNA registration for such sex offenders in conformity with the appearance schedule of SORNA § 116. In other words, sex offenders in these existing sex offender populations who cannot be registered within the normal SORNA time frame (i.e., before release from imprisonment or within three business days of sentencing for the registration offense) must be registered by the jurisdiction when it implements the SORNA requirements in its system within a year for sex offenders who satisfy the tier I criteria, within six months for sex offenders who satisfy the tier II criteria, and within three months for sex offenders who satisfy the tier III criteria. If a jurisdiction believes that it is not feasible for the jurisdiction to fully register the existing sex offender population in conformity with SORNA within these time frames, the jurisdiction should inform the SMART Office of the difficulty, and the SMART Office will consider whether an extension of time for implementation of SORNA under section 124(b) is warranted on that basis.

In cases in which a sex offender reenters the system based on conviction of some other offense—illustrated by the third example above—and is sentenced or released from imprisonment following the jurisdiction's implementation of SORNA, the normal SORNA initial registration procedures and timing requirements will apply, but with the new offense substituting for the predicate registration offense as the basis for the time frame. In other words, such a sex offender must be initially registered in the manner specified in SORNA § 117(a) prior to release from imprisonment for the new offense that brought him back into the system, or within three business days of sentencing for the new offense in case of a non-incarcerative sentence.

It may not always be possible to obtain information about earlier convictions of sex offenders in the classes described above, particularly when they occurred many years or decades ago, and available criminal history information may be uninformative as to factors such as victim age that can affect the nature and extent of registration requirements under SORNA. Jurisdictions may rely on the methods and standards they normally use in searching criminal records and on the information appearing in the records so obtained in carrying out the requirements described above to register sex offenders with pre-SORNA (or pre-SORNA-implementation) sex offense convictions.

FEDERAL AND MILITARY SEX OFFENDERS

There is no separate federal registration program for sex offenders required to register under SORNA who are released from federal or military custody. Rather, such sex offenders are integrated into the sex offender registration programs of the states and other (non-federal) jurisdictions following their release. Provisions of federal law, appearing in 18 U.S.C. 4042(c) and section 115(a)(8)(C) of Public Law 105-119, require federal and military correctional and supervision personnel to notify the receiving jurisdiction's authorities concerning the release to their areas of such sex offenders so that this integration can be effected. Moreover, these sex offenders are required to comply with the SORNA registration requirements in the jurisdictions in which they reside, are employed, or attend school as mandatory conditions of their federal supervision, as provided in 18 U.S.C. 3563(a)(8), 3583(d), 4209(a), and may be prosecuted under 18 U.S.C. 2250 if they fail to do so.

For example, consider a person convicted of aggravated sexual abuse under 18 U.S.C.

2241, who is released following his completion of the prison term for this offense. As provided in 18 U.S.C. 4042(c), the Federal Bureau of Prisons is required to inform the sex offender prior to his release that he must register as required by SORNA, and it notifies law enforcement and registration authorities in the jurisdiction in which the sex offender will reside following release.

Situations of this type are in principle the same as those in which a sex offender enters a jurisdiction to reside following conviction in another (non-federal) jurisdiction—*see* Part X of these Guidelines for discussion—except that the federal authorities will not have registered the sex offender in the same manner that a non-federal jurisdiction would. The jurisdiction to which such a sex offender goes to reside following release from federal custody (or after sentencing for a federal offense, in case of a non-incarcerative sentence) accordingly must require the sex offender to appear in person to register within three business days, and must carry out the procedure described in SORNA § 117(a) when the sex offender appears for that purpose. The jurisdiction must also immediately forward the registration information for the sex offender to any other jurisdiction in which the sex offender is required to register under SORNA (e.g., on the basis of employment), as required by SORNA §121(b)(3). If federal authorities notify the jurisdiction concerning the release of a sex offender to the jurisdiction, but the sex offender fails to appear and register as required, the jurisdiction must proceed as discussed in Part XIII of these Guidelines for cases involving possible violations of registration requirements.

SEX OFFENDERS INCARCERATED IN NON-CONVICTION JURISDICTIONS

A sex offender sentenced to imprisonment may serve his or her prison term in a facility outside of the convicting jurisdiction. For example, an Indian tribe may not have its own correctional facility and may accordingly lease bed space from a county jail. Or a state may lease prison space in a facility in an adjacent state, so that some of its offenders serve their prison terms in the other state's facilities. In such a case, the jurisdiction incarcerating the sex offender may be neither the jurisdiction of conviction nor the jurisdiction of expected residence following release. But it is likely to be in the best position to initially take the required registration information from the sex offender and to instruct the sex offender concerning registration obligations, while the jurisdiction that convicted the sex offender may be in no position to do so prior to the sex offender's release, because the facility in which the sex offender is incarcerated is in another jurisdiction.

In such cases, the jurisdiction incarcerating the sex offender must carry out the initial registration procedure described in SORNA § 117(a) prior to releasing the sex offender and must immediately forward the registration information for the sex offender to any other jurisdiction in which the sex offender is required to register under SORNA (e.g., on the basis of expected residence), as required by SORNA § 121(b)(3).

REGISTRANTS BASED ON FOREIGN CONVICTIONS

Persons with foreign sex offense convictions are often required to register under SORNA, as discussed in Part IV.B of these Guidelines. Section 128 of SORNA directs the Attorney General, in consultation with the Secretary of State and the Secretary of Homeland Security, to establish a system for informing the relevant jurisdictions about persons entering the United States who are required to register under SORNA. Persons with foreign sex offense convictions provide an additional class who cannot be initially registered within the normal SORNA time frame. Since they are convicted and imprisoned in a foreign country, no domestic jurisdiction would normally be in a position to register them prior to their release from imprisonment (or near the time of sentencing in case of a non-incarcerative sentence).

The procedure for initial registration of such persons is logically the same as that for other analogous classes discussed above: A jurisdiction must require a person with a foreign conviction for which registration is required under SORNA to appear in person to register within three business days of entering the jurisdiction to reside or commencing employment or school attendance in the jurisdiction. If the sex offender has not previously been registered by another jurisdiction, the jurisdiction must carry out the initial registration procedure as provided in SORNA § 117(a) when the sex offender appears. The jurisdiction must immediately forward the registration information to any other jurisdiction in which the sex offender is required to register under SORNA. If a jurisdiction is notified, by federal authorities pursuant to SORNA § 128 or otherwise, that a sex offender is entering the United States and is expected to be locating in the jurisdiction, but the sex offender fails to appear and register as required, the jurisdiction must follow the procedures discussed in Part XIII of these Guidelines for cases involving possible violations of registration requirements.

X.   KEEPING THE REGISTRATION CURRENT

There are a number of provisions in SORNA that are designed to ensure that changes in registration information are promptly reported, and that the registration information is kept fully up to date in all jurisdictions in which the sex offender is required to register:

- Section 113(a) provides that a sex offender must keep the registration current in each jurisdiction in which the sex offender resides, is an employee, or is a student.

- Section 113(c) provides that a sex offender must, not later than three business days after each change of name, residence, employment, or student status, appear in person in at least one jurisdiction in which the sex offender is required to register and inform that jurisdiction of all changes in the information required for that sex offender in the sex offender registry. It further provides that that information must immediately be provided to all other jurisdictions in which the sex offender is required to register.

- Section 119(b) provides that updated information about a sex offender must be immediately transmitted by electronic forwarding to all relevant jurisdictions.

- Section 121(b)(3) provides that immediately after a sex offender registers or updates a registration, the information in the registry (other than any exempted from disclosure by the Attorney General) must be provided to each jurisdiction where the sex offender resides, is an employee, or is a student, and each jurisdiction from or to which a change of residence, employment, or student status occurs.

- Section 128 directs the Attorney General, in consultation with the Secretary of State and the Secretary of Homeland Security, to establish a system for informing relevant jurisdictions about persons entering the United States who are required to register under SORNA.

Implementation of these provisions requires the definition of implementation measures that can be carried out by the individual jurisdictions, whose collective effect will be to realize these provisions' objectives. The remainder of this Part of these Guidelines details the required implementation measures.

A. Changes of Name, Residence, Employment, or School Attendance

The in-person appearance requirements of section 113(c) described above serve to ensure—in connection with the most substantial types of changes bearing on the identification or location of sex offenders (name, residence, employment, school attendance)—that there will be an opportunity to obtain all required registration information from sex offenders in an up to date form, including direct meetings for this purpose between the sex offenders and the personnel or agencies who will be responsible for their registration. The purposes served by in-person appearances under the SORNA standards are further explained in Part XI of these Guidelines, in relation to the periodic in-person appearance requirements of section 116.

The required implementation measures for the appearances required by section 113(c)—and other information updating/sharing and enforcement provisions under SORNA as they bear on such appearances—are as follows:

- RESIDENCE JURISDICTIONS: Each jurisdiction must require a sex offender who enters the jurisdiction to reside, or who is registered in the jurisdiction as a resident and changes his or her name or place of residence within the jurisdiction, to appear in person to register or update the registration within three business days. Also, each jurisdiction in which a sex offender is registered as a resident must:

  - require the sex offender to inform the jurisdiction if the sex offender intends to commence residence, employment, or school attendance in another jurisdiction; and

  - if so informed by the sex offender, notify that other jurisdiction by transmitting the sex offender's registration information (including the information concerning the sex offender's expected residence, employment, or school attendance in that jurisdiction) immediately by electronic forwarding to that jurisdiction.

- EMPLOYMENT JURISDICTIONS: Each jurisdiction must require a sex offender who commences employment in the jurisdiction, or changes employer or place of employment in the jurisdiction, to appear in person to register or update the registration within three business days.

50

- SCHOOL JURISDICTIONS: Each jurisdiction must require a sex offender who commences school attendance in the jurisdiction, or changes the school attended or place of school attendance in the jurisdiction, to appear in person to register or update the registration within three business days.

- INFORMATION SHARING: In all cases in which a sex offender makes an in-person appearance in a jurisdiction and registers or updates a registration as described above, the jurisdiction must immediately transmit by electronic forwarding the registration information for the sex offender (including any updated information concerning name, residence, employment, or school attendance provided in the appearance) to all other jurisdictions in which:

  ○ the sex offender is or will be required to register as a resident, employee, or student; or

  ○ the sex offender was required to register as a resident, employee, or student until the time of a change of residence, employment, or student status reported in the appearance, even if the sex offender may no longer be required to register in that jurisdiction in light of the change of residence, employment, or student status.

- FAILURE TO APPEAR: If a jurisdiction is notified that a sex offender is expected to commence residence, employment, or school attendance in the jurisdiction, but the sex offender fails to appear for registration as required, the jurisdiction must inform the jurisdiction that provided the notification that the sex offender failed to appear, and must follow the procedures for cases involving possible violations of registration requirements, as discussed in Part XIII of these Guidelines.

Defining changes in such matters as residence and employment may present special difficulties in relation to sex offenders who lack fixed residence or employment. For example, a homeless sex offender may sleep on a different park bench each night. Or the employer of a sex offender who does day labor, working for whatever contractor hires him on a given day, may change on a daily basis. In such cases, a jurisdiction is not required to treat all such changes as changes in residence or employment status that bring into play the requirement to conduct an in-person appearance within three business days for purposes of reporting the change. Rather, as discussed in Part VI of these Guidelines, the information in the registry describing the places of residence or employment for sex offenders who lack fixed residence or employment may be in more general terms, and jurisdictions may limit their reporting requirements to changes that would entail some modification of the registry information relating to these matters.

In one respect, the foregoing procedures for updating registration information through in-person appearances do not fully ensure that registrations will be kept current with respect to residence, employment, and school attendance information, because they relate to situations in which future information about these matters is available. But that is not always the case. For example, a transient sex offender may be leaving the jurisdiction in which he is registered as a resident, but may be unable to say where he will be living thereafter. Or a sex offender registered as an employee or student in a jurisdiction may quit his job or leave school, but may have no prospect for subsequent employment or education at the time. If such changes were not reported, the affected jurisdictions' registries would not be kept current, but rather would contain outdated information showing sex offenders to be residing, employed, or attending school in places where they no longer are. Accordingly, a jurisdiction in which a sex offender is registered as a resident, employee, or student must also require the sex offender to inform the jurisdiction if the sex offender is terminating residence, employment, or school attendance in the jurisdiction, even if there is no ascertainable or expected future place of residence, employment, or school attendance for the sex offender.

B. Changes in Other Registration Information

By incorporating the foregoing procedures into their registration programs, jurisdictions can implement the SORNA requirements for keeping the registration current in relation to name, residence, employment, and school attendance information. The registration information that sex offenders are required to provide under SORNA § 114, however, as discussed in Part VI of these Guidelines, includes as well information about vehicles owned or operated by sex offenders, temporary lodging information—i.e., information about any place in which a sex offender is staying when away from his residence for seven or more days—and information about designations that sex offenders use for self-identification or routing purposes in Internet communications or postings or telephonic communications. If changes occur in these types of information, the changes may eventually be reported as part of the periodic verification appearances required by section 116 of SORNA, as discussed in Part XI of these Guidelines. But the registration information may become in some respects seriously out of date if the verification appearances are relied on exclusively for this purpose.

For example, if a sex offender is on a yearly appearance schedule, the sex offender's motor vehicle information may be a year out of date by the time the sex offender reports at the next appearance that he has acquired a new vehicle. Temporary lodging at places away from a sex offender's residence might not be reported until long after the time when the sex offender was at the temporary location. Likewise, given the ease with which Internet addresses and identifiers and telephone numbers are added, dropped, or changed, the value of requiring information about them from registrants could be seriously undermined if they were only required to report changes periodically in the context of general verification meetings.

Hence, an additional implementation measure is necessary to keep registrations current with respect to these informational items:

- Each jurisdiction in which a sex offender is registered as a resident must require the sex offender to report immediately changes in vehicle information, temporary lodging information, and changes in designations used for self-identification or routing in Internet communications or postings or telephonic communications, and must immediately transmit such changes in the registration information by electronic forwarding to all other jurisdictions in which the sex offender is required to register.

52

- In addition, with respect to temporary lodging information, the residence jurisdiction must immediately transmit the information by electronic forwarding to the jurisdiction in which the temporary lodging by the sex offender takes place (if different from the residence jurisdiction), even if that is not a jurisdiction in which the sex offender is required to register.

C. International Travel

A sex offender who moves to a foreign country may pass beyond the reach of U.S. jurisdictions and hence may not be subject to any enforceable registration requirement under U.S. law unless and until he or she returns to the United States. But effective tracking of such sex offenders remains a matter of concern to the United States and its domestic jurisdictions, and some measures relating to them are necessary for implementation of SORNA.

Relevant provisions include SORNA § 128, which directs the Attorney General to establish a system for informing domestic jurisdictions about persons entering the United States who are required to register under SORNA, and 18 U.S.C. 2250(a)(2)(B), which makes it a federal crime for a sex offender to travel in foreign commerce and knowingly fail to register or update a registration as required by SORNA. To carry out its responsibilities under these provisions, the Department of Justice needs to know if sex offenders registered in U.S. jurisdictions are leaving the country, since such offenders will be required to resume registration if they later return to the United States to live, work, or attend school while still within their registration periods. Also, both for sex offenders who are convicted in the United States and then go abroad, and for sex offenders who are initially convicted in other countries, identifying such sex offenders when they enter or reenter the United States will require cooperative efforts between the Department of Justice (including the United States Marshals Service) and agencies of foreign countries. As a necessary part of such cooperative activities, foreign authorities may expect U.S. authorities to inform them about sex offenders coming to their jurisdictions from the United States, in return for their advising the United States about sex offenders coming to the United States from their jurisdictions. For this reason as well, federal authorities in the United States will need information about sex offenders leaving domestic jurisdictions to go abroad in order to effectively carry out the requirements of SORNA § 128 and enforce 18 U.S.C. 2250(a)(2)(B).

International travel also implicates the requirement of SORNA § 113(a) that sex offenders keep the registration current in all jurisdictions in which they reside, work, or attend school. If a sex offender simply leaves the country and does not inform the jurisdiction or jurisdictions in which he has been registered, then the requirement to keep the registration current will not have been fulfilled. Rather, the registry information in the domestic jurisdictions will show that the sex offender is residing in the jurisdiction (or present as an employee or student) when that is no longer the case.

In addition, a sex offender who goes abroad may remain subject in some respects to U.S. jurisdiction. For example, a sex offender may be leaving to live on an overseas U.S. military base, as a service member, dependent, or employee, or to work as or for a U.S. military contractor in another country. In such cases, notification about the individual's status as a sex offender and intended activities abroad is of interest to federal authorities, because the presence of sex offenders implicates the same public safety concerns in relation to communities abroad for which the United States has responsibility (such as U.S. military base communities in foreign countries) as it does in relation to communities within the United States.

The following requirements accordingly apply in relation to sex offenders who leave the United States:

- Each jurisdiction in which a sex offender is registered as a resident must require the sex offender to inform the jurisdiction if the sex offender intends to commence residence, employment, or school attendance outside of the United States.

- If so informed by the sex offender, the jurisdiction must: (i) notify all other jurisdictions in which the sex offender is required to register through immediate electronic forwarding of the sex offender's registration information (including the information concerning the sex offender's expected residence, employment, or school attendance outside of the United States), and (ii) notify the United States Marshals Service and update the sex offender's registration information in the national databases pursuant to the procedures under SORNA § 121(b)(1).

SORNA does not require that all notifications to jurisdictions by sex offenders concerning changes in their registration information be made through in-person appearances. Rather, the in-person appearance requirement of SORNA § 113(c) relates to changes in name, and to changes in residence, employment, or school attendance between jurisdictions or within jurisdictions, which jurisdictions must require sex offenders to report through in-person appearances under the circumstances expressly identified in Subpart A of this Part. The means by which sex offenders are required to report other changes in registration information discussed in this Part are matters that jurisdictions may determine in their discretion.

XI.   VERIFICATION/APPEARANCE REQUIREMENTS

Section 116 of SORNA states that "[a] sex offender shall appear in person, allow the jurisdiction to take a current photograph, and verify the information in each registry in which that offender is required to be registered not less frequently than": (i) each year for a tier I sex offender, (ii) every six months for a tier II sex offender, and (iii) every three months for a tier III sex offender. Jurisdictions accordingly must require such periodic appearances by sex offenders who reside or are employees or students in the jurisdiction, since sex offenders must register in the jurisdictions of their residence, employment, and school attendance, as explained in Part VIII of these Guidelines. As with other SORNA requirements, jurisdictions may require in-person appearances by sex offenders with greater frequency than the minimum required by section 116.

The in-person appearance requirements of section 116 further the purposes of sex offender registration and notification in a number of ways. A sex offender's physical appearance, like that of any other person, will change in the course of time. The in-person appearance requirements provide reasonably frequent opportunities to obtain a photograph of the sex offender and a physical description that reflects his or her current appearance, types of registration information that are required by section 114(b)(1), (4). The in-person appearances further provide an opportunity to review with the sex offender the full range of information in the registry, and to obtain from the sex offender information about any changes in the registration information or new information that has not been reported since the initial registration or the last appearance.

Beyond these functions of directly helping to ensure the accuracy and currency of the registration information, the appearance requirement ensures periodic face-to-face encounters between the sex offender and persons responsible for his or her registration. For example, if the appearance requirement is implemented by a jurisdiction to require that registrants report to local police departments or sheriffs' offices, these meetings help to familiarize law enforcement personnel with the sex offenders in their areas. This may contribute to the effective discharge of the local law enforcement agency's protective and investigative functions in relation to these sex offenders, and help to ensure that the agency's responsibility to track these sex offenders is taken seriously and consistently enforced. Likewise, from the perspective of the sex offender, periodic in-person encounters with officials responsible for their monitoring may help to impress on them with greater vividness than remote communications that their identities, locations, and past criminal conduct are known to the authorities. Hence, there is a reduced likelihood of their avoiding detection and apprehension if they reoffend, and this may help them to resist the temptation to reoffend.

As long as the appearances involve meetings between the sex offenders and officials who can carry out the required functions of the meetings, the specific arrangements for such appearances and the officials who will conduct them are matters that jurisdictions may determine in their discretion. For example, jurisdictions may require sex offenders to report to local law enforcement offices for this purpose, or may combine the appearances with meetings between sex offenders and their supervision officers if they are under supervision, or may have law enforcement, supervision, or registration personnel visit with sex offenders at their homes or meet with them at other arranged locations.

The specific requirements for the conduct of such appearances are as follows:

- Appearances must be conducted at least annually for sex offenders satisfying the "tier I" criteria, at least semiannually for sex offenders satisfying the "tier II" criteria, and at least quarterly for sex offenders satisfying the "tier III" criteria. (The "tier" classifications and what they entail are explained in Part V of these Guidelines.)

- The sex offender must allow a current photograph to be taken. This does not mean that jurisdictions must require officials conducting these meetings to take a new photograph at every appearance and enter the new photograph into the registry. Where the official sees that the sex offender's appearance has not changed significantly from a photograph in the registry, it may be concluded that the existing photograph remains sufficiently current and the taking of a new photograph does not have to be required in such circumstances.

- The sex offender must be required to review the existing information in the registry that is within his or her knowledge, to correct any item that has changed or is otherwise inaccurate, and to provide any new information there may be in the required registration information categories.

- Upon entry of the updated information into the registry, it must be immediately transmitted by electronic forwarding to all other jurisdictions: (i) in which the sex offender is or will be required to register as a resident, employee, or student, or (ii) in which the sex offender was required to register as a resident, employee, or student until the time of a change of residence, employment, or student status reported in the appearance, even if the sex offender may no longer be required to register in that jurisdiction in light of the updated information. (This is necessary to carry out information sharing requirements appearing in SORNA §§ 119(b) and 121(b)(3).)

It may come to the attention of a jurisdiction's registration authorities that a sex offender has died when the sex offender fails to appear for a scheduled appearance under section 116 or by other means. While SORNA does not address the updating of registration information in such circumstances, jurisdictions are encouraged, as a matter of sound policy, to promptly update the information in the registry and the jurisdiction's public sex offender website to reflect the registrant's death, and to notify any other jurisdiction in which he was required to register. This does not necessarily mean, however, that all references to the sex offender should be removed from the registry and the website. Maintenance of historical information concerning a sex offender in the registry—together with the information that he is deceased—may remain of value, for example, in facilitating the solution of crimes he committed before his death by showing where he was at the time of the crimes. Likewise, maintenance of a public website posting for the sex offender (including the information that he is deceased) may remain of value since, for example, such a posting could enable victims of his crimes who have been checking on his status and location to ascertain that he is no longer alive.

Like other SORNA registration requirements, the in-person appearance requirements of section 116 are only minimum standards. They do not limit, and are not meant to discourage, adoption by jurisdictions of more extensive or additional measures for verifying registration information. Thus, jurisdictions may require verification of registration information with greater frequency than that required by section 116, and may wish to include in their systems additional means of verification for registration information, such as mailing address verification forms to the registered residence address that the sex offender is required to sign and return, and cross-checking information provided by the sex offender for inclusion in the registry against other records systems. Section 631 of the Adam Walsh Act (P.L. 109-248) authorizes a separate grant program to assist in residence address verification for sex offenders. Additional guidance will be provided concerning application for grants under that program if funding for the program becomes available.

XII.   DURATION OF REGISTRATION

Section 115(a) of SORNA specifies the minimum required duration of sex offender registration. It generally requires that sex offenders keep the registration current for 15 years in case of a tier I sex offender, for 25 years in case of a tier II sex offender, and for the life of the sex offender in case of a tier III sex offender, "excluding any time the sex offender is in custody or civilly committed." (The tier classifications and their import are explained in Part V of these Guidelines.) The required registration period begins to run upon release from custody for a sex offender sentenced to incarceration for the registration offense, and begins to run at the time of sentencing for a sex offender who receives a nonincarcerative sentence for the offense.

The proviso relating to custody or civil commitment reflects the fact that the SORNA procedures for keeping up the registration—including appearances to report changes of residence or other key information under section 113(c), and periodic appearances for verification under section 116—generally presuppose the case of a sex offender who is free in the community. Where a sex offender is confined, the public is protected against the risk of his reoffending in a more direct way, and more certain means are available for tracking his whereabouts. Hence, SORNA does not require that jurisdictions apply the registration procedures applicable to sex offenders in the community during periods in which a sex offender is in custody or civilly committed.

However, jurisdictions are not required to "toll" the running of the registration period during such subsequent periods of confinement. For example, consider a sex offender released from imprisonment in 2010 who is subject to 25 years of registration under the SORNA standards as a tier II offender, where the sex offender is subsequently convicted during the registration period for committing a robbery and imprisoned for three years for that offense. If the jurisdiction would otherwise require the sex offender to register until 2035 (the 25 year SORNA minimum), it may wish to extend that to 2038 so that the three years the sex offender spent in prison for the robbery is effectively not credited towards the running of the registration period. But that is a matter in the jurisdiction's discretion. Terminating the registration in 2035 would also be consistent with SORNA's requirements.

Subsection (b) of section 115 allows the registration period to be reduced by 5 years for a tier I sex offender who has maintained a "clean record" for 10 years, and allows registration to be terminated for a tier III sex offender required to register on the basis of a juvenile delinquency adjudication if the sex offender has maintained a "clean record" for 25 years. (The circumstances in which registration is required on the basis of juvenile delinquency adjudications are explained in Part IV.A of these Guidelines.) There is no authorization to reduce the required 25-year duration of registration for tier II sex offenders, or to reduce the required lifetime registration for tier III sex offenders required to register on the basis of adult convictions.

The specific requirements under section 115(b) to satisfy the "clean record" precondition for reduction of the registration period are as follows:

- The sex offender must not be convicted of any offense for which imprisonment for more than one year may be imposed (§ 115(b)(1)(A)).

- The sex offender must not be convicted of any sex offense (§ 115(b)(1)(B)). In contrast to section 115(b)(1)(A), section 115(b)(1)(B) is not limited to cases in which the offense is one potentially punishable by imprisonment for more than a year. Hence, conviction for a sex offense prevents satisfaction of the "clean record" requirement, even if the maximum penalty for the offense is less than a year.

• The sex offender must successfully complete any periods of supervised release, probation, and parole (§ 115(b)(1)(C)). The requirement of "successfully" completing periods of supervision means completing these periods without revocation.

• The sex offender must successfully complete an appropriate sex offender treatment program certified by a jurisdiction or by the Attorney General (§ 115(b)(1)(D)). Jurisdictions may make their own decisions concerning the design of such treatment programs, and jurisdictions may choose the criteria to be applied in determining whether a sex offender has "successfully" completed a treatment program, which may involve relying on the professional judgment of the persons who conduct or oversee the treatment program.

XIII. ENFORCEMENT OF REGISTRATION REQUIREMENTS

This final part of the Guidelines discusses enforcement of registration requirements under the SORNA provisions. It initially discusses the penalties for registration violations under SORNA, and then the practical procedures for investigating and dealing with such violations.

SORNA contemplates that substantial criminal penalties will be available for registration violations at the state, local, and federal levels. Section 113(e) of SORNA requires jurisdictions (other than Indian tribes) to provide a criminal penalty that includes a maximum term of imprisonment greater than one year for the failure of a sex offender to comply with the SORNA requirements. Hence, a jurisdiction's implementation of SORNA includes having a failure-to-register offense for which the maximum authorized term of imprisonment exceeds a year. (Indian tribes are not included in this requirement because tribal court jurisdiction does not extend to imposing terms of imprisonment exceeding a year.) Section 141(a) of SORNA enacted 18 U.S.C. 2250, a new federal failure-to-register offense, which provides federal criminal penalties of up to 10 years of imprisonment for sex offenders required to register under SORNA who knowingly fail to register or update a registration as required where circumstances supporting federal jurisdiction exist, such as interstate or international travel by a sex offender, or conviction of a federal sex offense for which registration is required. Federal sex offenders are also required to comply with the SORNA registration requirements as mandatory conditions of their federal probation, supervised release, or parole, as provided pursuant to amendments adopted by section 141(d)-(e), (j) of SORNA.

In terms of practical enforcement measures, SORNA § 122 requires that an appropriate official notify the Attorney General and appropriate law enforcement agencies of failures by sex offenders to comply with registration requirements, and that such registration violations must be reflected in the registries. The section further provides that the official, the Attorney General, and each such law enforcement agency are to take any appropriate action to ensure compliance.

58

Complementary measures for federal enforcement appear in section 142, which directs the Attorney General to use the resources of federal law enforcement, including the United States Marshals Service, to assist jurisdictions in locating and apprehending sex offenders who violate registration requirements. (Also, SORNA § 623 authorizes grants by the Attorney General to states, local governments, tribal governments, and other public and private entities to assist in enforcing sex offender registration requirements—additional guidance will be provided concerning application for grants under this provision if funding is made available for this program.)

Translating the requirements of section 122 into practical procedures that will ensure effective enforcement of sex offender registration requires further definition. Jurisdictions can implement the requirements of section 122 by adopting the following procedures:

- Information may be received by a jurisdiction indicating that a sex offender has absconded—i.e., has not registered at all, or has moved to some unknown place other than the registered place of residence. For example, a sex offender may fail to make a scheduled appearance for periodic verification of registration information in his jurisdiction of residence as required by SORNA § 116, or may fail to return an address verification form mailed to the registered address in a jurisdiction that uses that verification procedure. Or a jurisdiction may receive notice from some other jurisdiction providing grounds to expect that a sex offender will be coming to live in the jurisdiction—such as notice that a sex offender will be moving to the jurisdiction from a jurisdiction in which he was previously registered, or notice from federal authorities about the expected arrival in the jurisdiction of a released federal sex offender or sex offender entering the United States from abroad—but the sex offender then fails to appear and register as required. Or a jurisdiction may notify another jurisdiction, based on information provided by a sex offender, that the sex offender will be relocating to the other jurisdiction, but the supposed destination jurisdiction thereafter informs the original registration jurisdiction that the sex offender has failed to appear and register.

- When such information is received by a jurisdiction indicating that a sex offender may have absconded, whether one registered in the jurisdiction or expected to arrive from another jurisdiction, an effort must be made to determine whether the sex offender has actually absconded. If non-law enforcement registration personnel cannot determine this, then a law enforcement agency with jurisdiction to investigate the matter must be notified. Also, if the information indicating the possible absconding came through notice from another jurisdiction or federal authorities, the authorities that provided the notification must be informed that the sex offender has failed to appear and register.

- If a jurisdiction receives information indicating that a sex offender may have absconded, as described in the preceding bullets, and takes the measures described therein but cannot locate the sex offender, then the jurisdiction must take the following steps:

  ○ The information in the registry must be revised to reflect that the sex offender is an absconder or unlocatable.

- A warrant must be sought for the sex offender's arrest, if the legal requirements for doing so are satisfied.

- The United States Marshals Service, which is the lead federal agency for investigating sex offender registration violations, must be notified. Also, the jurisdiction must update the National Sex Offender Registry to reflect the sex offender's status as an absconder or unlocatable and enter the sex offender into the National Crime Information Center Wanted Person File (assuming issuance of a warrant meeting the requirement for entry into that file).

The foregoing procedures must be adopted for possible absconder cases to implement SORNA § 122. In addition, a jurisdiction's policies must require appropriate follow-up measures when information is received indicating violation of the requirement to register in jurisdictions of employment or school attendance, whether or not a violation of the requirement to register in jurisdictions of residence is implicated. Specifically, a jurisdiction may receive information indicating that a sex offender may be employed or attending school in the jurisdiction but has not registered as required—for example, failure by the sex offender to appear for a required periodic in-person appearance in the employment or school jurisdiction, as required by SORNA § 116, or failure by a sex offender to appear and register in the jurisdiction following receipt of notice from another jurisdiction that the sex offender is expected to be commencing employment or school attendance in the jurisdiction. In such cases, an effort must be made to determine whether the sex offender is actually employed or attending school in the jurisdiction but has failed to register. If (non-law enforcement) registration personnel cannot determine this, then a law enforcement agency with jurisdiction to investigate the matter must be notified.

_____

Date

_____

Michael B. Mukasey

Attorney General

Appendix A. Summary of Comments

DEPARTMENT OF JUSTICE

[Docket No. OAG 121; AG Order No. 2978-2008]

RIN 1105-AB28

Office of the Attorney General; The National Guidelines for

Sex Offender Registration and Notification

AGENCY: Department of Justice.

ACTION: Final guidelines.

SUMMARY: The United States Department of Justice is publishing Final Guidelines to interpret and implement the Sex Offender Registration and Notification Act.

EFFECTIVE DATE: July 2, 2008.

FOR FURTHER INFORMATION CONTACT: Laura L. Rogers, Director, SMART Office, Office of Justice Programs, United States Department of Justice, Washington, DC, phone: 202-514-4689, e-mail: Getsmart@usdoj.gov.

SUPPLEMENTARY INFORMATION: Since the enactment of the Jacob Wetterling Crimes Against Children and Sexually Violent Offender Registration Act (42 U.S.C. 14071) in 1994, there have been national standards for sex offender registration and notification in the United States. All states currently have sex offender registration and notification programs and have endeavored to implement the Wetterling Act standards in their existing programs.

Title I of the Adam Walsh Child Protection and Safety Act of 2006 (Pub. L. 109-248), the Sex Offender Registration and Notification Act (SORNA), contains a comprehensive revision of the national standards for sex offender registration and notification. The SORNA reforms are generally designed to strengthen and increase the effectiveness of sex offender registration and notification for the protection of the public, and to eliminate potential gaps and loopholes under the pre-existing standards by means of which sex offenders could attempt to evade registration requirements or the consequences of registration violations.

Section 112(b) of SORNA (42 U.S.C. 16912(b)) directs the Attorney General to issue guidelines to interpret and implement SORNA. The Department of Justice published proposed guidelines in the Federal Register on May 30, 2007, for this purpose. *See* 72 FR 30209 (May 30, 2007). The comment period ended on August 1, 2007.

These final guidelines provide guidance and assistance to the states and other jurisdictions in incorporating the SORNA requirements into their sex offender registration and notification programs. Matters addressed in the guidelines include general principles for SORNA implementation; the jurisdictions responsible for implementing the SORNA standards in their programs; the sex offenders required to register under SORNA and the registration and notification requirements they are subject to based on the nature of their offenses and the extent of their recidivism; the information to be included in the sex offender registries and the disclosure and sharing of such information; the jurisdictions in which sex offenders are required to register; the procedures for initially registering sex offenders and for keeping the registration current and the registration information up to date; the duration of registration; and the means of enforcing registration requirements.

A summary of the comments received on the proposed guidelines follows, including discussion of changes in the final guidelines based on the comments received, followed by the text of the final guidelines.

Summary of Comments on the Proposed Guidelines

Approximately 275 comments were received on the proposed guidelines. The Department of Justice appreciates the interest and insight reflected in the many submissions and communications, and has considered them carefully. In general, the comments did not show a need to change the overall character of the guidelines, but in some areas the commenters provided persuasive reasons to change the proposed guidelines' treatment of significant issues, or pointed to a need to provide further clarification about them.

The initial portion of this summary reviews the most significant and most common issues raised in the comments, and identifies changes made in the final guidelines relating to these issues. The remainder of the summary thereafter runs through the provisions of the guidelines in the order in which they appear, and discusses in greater detail the comments on each topical area in the guidelines and changes made (or not made) on the basis of public comments.

Tribal issues: Comments were received from a number of Indian tribal organizations and individual tribes that expressed their strong commitment to the protection of their communities from sex offenders through effective registration and notification. These comments, however, emphasized the importance of consulting and involving tribal representatives in all aspects of SORNA implementation affecting tribal interests, and presented well-founded proposals for changing a number of provisions in the guidelines. Specific changes in the final guidelines based on these comments include: (i) clarifying that groups of tribes may enter into cooperative arrangements among themselves to effect the substantial implementation of the SORNA requirements, (ii) striking a provision of the proposed guidelines that was seen as according less respect to tribal sex offense convictions than to sex offense convictions in other jurisdictions, and (iii) modifying a requirement for sex offenders to register ethnic or tribal names whose formulation was overly broad in the proposed guidelines. The comments received on tribal issues and resulting changes in the final guidelines are further discussed below in connection with § 127 of SORNA, the meaning of "conviction" for purposes of SORNA, and required registration information under SORNA.

Treatment of juveniles: Comments were received from various groups and individuals objecting to SORNA's treatment of juvenile delinquents. The relevant SORNA provisions require registration for juveniles at least 14 years old who are adjudicated delinquent for committing particularly serious sexually assaultive crimes (offenses "comparable to aggravated sexual abuse"). These comments could not be accommodated in the guidelines to the extent that they simply express disagreement with the legislative decision in SORNA § 111(8) that a narrowly defined class of juvenile delinquents should be subject to SORNA's requirements, or propose that jurisdictions be deemed to have substantially implemented SORNA even if they globally dispense with SORNA's registration and notification requirements in relation to juveniles. However, the comments have provided grounds for further thought about the implementation of § 111(8)'s requirement that juveniles at least age 14 adjudicated delinquent for offenses comparable to aggravated sexual abuse be registered, resulting in a substantial change in the final guidelines' treatment of this issue. As revised, the guidelines explain that it is sufficient for substantial implementation of this aspect of SORNA to require registration for (roughly speaking) juveniles at least age 14 who are adjudicated delinquent for offenses equivalent to rape or attempted rape, but not for those adjudicated delinquent for lesser sexual assaults or non-violent sexual conduct. The comments received on this issue and the changes made on the basis of the comments are further discussed below in connection with the "substantial implementation" standard under SORNA and in connection with SORNA's concept of "conviction" (parts II.E and IV.A of the guidelines).

Retroactivity: Some commenters objected to, or expressed concerns about, provisions of the guidelines that require that jurisdictions apply the SORNA requirements "retroactively" to certain categories of offenders whose sex offense convictions predate the enactment of SORNA or its implementation in a particular jurisdiction. The guidelines specifically require registering in conformity with SORNA sex offenders who remain in the system as prisoners, supervisees, or registrants, or who reenter the system through a subsequent criminal conviction. Some comments of this type opined that Congress was simply wrong in enacting SORNA's requirements for sex offender registration and notification, and that the Attorney General should mitigate the resulting harm by defining their scope of application as narrowly as possible. This premise cannot be accepted or acted on in issuing guidelines to "interpret and implement" SORNA, as SORNA § 112(b) requires the Attorney General to do. Other commenters, however, expressed concerns of a more practical nature, based on potential difficulties in finding older convictions and determining whether registration is required for them under SORNA's standards. The final guidelines address this concern by clarifying that jurisdictions may rely on their normal methods and standards in searching criminal records for this purpose, and that information about underlying offense conduct or circumstances does not have to be sought beyond that appearing in available criminal history information. Parallel explanation has also been provided in relation to pre-SORNA (or pre-SORNA-implementation) convictions that raise a sex offender's tier classification under SORNA on grounds of recidivism.

Information subject to website posting: Some state officials who submitted comments expressed concern that their jurisdictions would be required to post various types of registration information on their public sex offender websites—e.g., fingerprints, palm prints, and DNA information—that would be of no real interest to the public or inappropriate for public disclosure. However, the guidelines identify a limited number of informational items concerning a sex offender that must be included on the websites—in essence, name information, address information, vehicle information, physical description, sex offenses for which convicted, and a current photograph—and do not require website posting of registration information outside of these categories. The guidelines in their final formulation have been revised for greater clarity concerning the information that must be included on jurisdictions' sex offender websites and the information that need not be included.

Registration jurisdictions: Some commenters raised questions about in-state registration requirements, such as whether a sex offender who resides in one county and is employed in another would have to register in both counties. The answer is that this is a matter of state discretion. The "jurisdictions" in which SORNA requires registration are the 50 States, the five principal territories, the District of Columbia, and Indian tribes that have elected to be registration jurisdictions in conformity with § 127—the definition does not cover counties, cities, towns, or other political subdivisions of states or other covered jurisdictions. SORNA § 113(a) provides that sex offenders must register in the jurisdictions (as so defined) in which they live, work, or attend school, but SORNA does not prescribe finer requirements as to the particular area(s) or location(s) within individual states, territories, or tribes where sex offenders must register or make in-person appearances. Questions were also raised whether there is a continuing registration requirement under SORNA—beyond initial registration—in relation to the jurisdiction in which a sex offender was originally convicted for the registration offense, if the sex offender does not reside, work, or attend school in that jurisdiction. The answer is no. While SORNA itself (§§ 111(10), 113(a)) and the proposed guidelines reflect these points, some additional explicit language has been added about them in the final guidelines to foreclose future misunderstandings of this type.

Offense of conviction versus underlying conduct: Some commenters raised questions or provided recommendations as to whether the application of SORNA's requirements depends on the elements of the offense for which the sex offender is convicted or the underlying offense conduct. The answer to this question may affect whether registration is required by SORNA at all, and may affect the "tier" classification of offenders under the SORNA standards. The general answer is that jurisdictions are not required by SORNA to look beyond the elements of the offense of conviction in determining registration requirements, except with respect to victim age. The discussion of the tier classifications has been edited in the final guidelines to make this point more clearly.

Duration of registration: Some commenters expressed uncertainties or criticisms relating to provisions in the guidelines affecting the duration of registration. The matters raised included (i) whether the running of the registration period is suspended by the subsequent incarceration of the sex offender or other subsequent events (tolling), and (ii) the conditions for reducing registration periods. The discussion of these issues has been revised in some respects in the final guidelines for greater clarity.

Risk assessments: Some commenters asked whether a jurisdiction could be considered to have substantially implemented the SORNA requirements if the jurisdiction globally dispensed with those requirements and instead based sex offender registration or notification on individualized risk assessments of sex offenders. The answer is no, for reasons that are further discussed in connection with "substantial implementation" later in this summary. This does not mean, however, that SORNA bars jurisdictions from utilizing risk assessments in their systems if they so wish. Jurisdictions may have reasons for carrying out such assessments independent of registration/notification issues, such as to inform decisions concerning the conditions or duration of supervision, and they remain free to utilize such assessments as a basis for prescribing registration or notification requirements that exceed the minimum required by SORNA. For example, there is no inconsistency with SORNA if a jurisdiction prescribes a longer registration period or more frequent verification appearances than the minimum required under SORNA §§ 111(2)-(4), 115-16, based on a risk assessment indicating that a sex offender is at "high risk" of reoffending, or if a jurisdiction includes on its public sex offender website information showing the results of risk assessments of individual offenders.

Aids to implementation: Some of the commenters recommended the development of practical information technology and documentary tools to facilitate SORNA implementation. Various measures of this sort will be pursued. The final guidelines themselves will be available in a more user-friendly form on the SMART Office website, which will include a table of contents with page number references and an index. Per the directive in SORNA § 123, software is being developed and communications systems arrangements are being made that will facilitate the interjurisdictional exchange of registration information, automate the posting of information to sex offender websites and the operation of such websites in conformity with the SORNA requirements, and otherwise enable jurisdictions to implement the SORNA requirements in their programs as far as possible by using these technological tools. Additional implementation tools the SMART Office is developing include: a database of statutes ranging back to approximately 1960 for all SORNA jurisdictions, which jurisdictions will be able to link to from their registries to provide the text of the conviction offense for each registered sex offender; a statutory matrix of sex offense provisions from all SORNA jurisdictions, which will assist jurisdictions in ascertaining the SORNA registration and notification requirements applicable to offenders convicted of these offenses; checklists that jurisdictions will be able to use to evaluate whether the SORNA requirements are met in their programs and to structure their submissions to the SMART Office establishing SORNA implementation; model forms that jurisdictions will be able to use to inform sex offenders about their obligations under SORNA; and model templates for jurisdictions to use to create cooperative agreements.

Jurisdiction-specific questions: Some commenters—particularly state officials with responsibilities relating to sex offender registration or notification—submitted extensive questions, comments, and observations relating to the implementation of SORNA in their jurisdictions. This summary does not attempt to provide an exhaustive account of such submissions, or to respond to them point by point. The number of specific questions or comments of this type is very large and many of them relate to matters that may not arise in, and may not be of interest to, jurisdictions other than the particular jurisdiction that submitted the questions. Also, these comments largely did not propose changes in the guidelines, but perhaps sought confirmation of the guidelines' meaning in relation to certain matters, or practical advice or suggestions for implementing the SORNA requirements in particular state systems. The SMART Office's cooperative work with all jurisdictions in their SORNA implementation efforts will provide a more satisfactory means of answering questions and addressing matters of this type than this summary of comments on the proposed SORNA implementation guidelines.

Residency restrictions and other misunderstandings: A number of commenters submitted critical comments concerning supposed requirements that do not appear in SORNA or the guidelines. For example, some commenters complained that SORNA or the guidelines would prevent sex offenders from living in many areas. But SORNA's requirements are informational in nature and do not restrict where sex offenders can live. To the extent that states, other SORNA jurisdictions, or municipalities prescribe restrictions on areas that sex offenders may enter or reside in, it is a matter in their discretion, and any objections to such restrictions would need to be addressed to the governmental entities that adopt them. As a second example, some commenters assumed that there is little or no difference between the treatment of adult sex offenders and juveniles under SORNA and the guidelines, and that SORNA would require registration by teenagers based on consensual sexual conduct with other teenagers of similar age. No changes have been made in the guidelines on the basis of such comments because they involve incorrect assumptions concerning matters that SORNA and the guidelines do not require.

Objections to SORNA: Some of the comments stated objections to SORNA generally, to specific sex offender registration or notification requirements prescribed by SORNA, or to features of the guidelines that straightforwardly reflect SORNA's requirements. Changes have not been made in the guidelines based on such comments because the Attorney General has no authority to repeal or overrule the national standards for sex offender registration and notification that are embodied in SORNA. Rather, the Attorney General's responsibility is to interpret and implement those standards in the guidelines, as required by SORNA § 112(b).

The remainder of this summary discusses comments received on the guidelines' provisions in the order in which those provisions appear in the guidelines.

I.   Introduction

No comments were received that provided any persuasive reason to change the Introduction, and it remains the same in the final guidelines.

II.   General Principles

A. Terminology

The proposed guidelines, following the express definition in SORNA § 111(10), used the term "jurisdictions" to refer to the 50 States, the District of Columbia, the five principal U.S.

territories, and Indian tribes so qualifying under § 127. Some comments received nevertheless reflected a misunderstanding of "jurisdictions" in some contexts in the guidelines as including

political subdivisions of states (e.g., counties). Additional explanation about the meaning of "jurisdiction" has been added in the "terminology" section in the final guidelines to foreclose misunderstandings of this type. A paragraph has also been added explaining the use of the term "imprisonment" in SORNA and the guidelines.

B. Minimum National Standards

The proposed guidelines stated that SORNA generally establishes *minimum* national standards, setting a floor, not a ceiling, for jurisdictions' sex offender registration and notification programs. Hence, jurisdictions may adopt requirements that encompass the SORNA baseline of sex offender registration and notification requirements but exceed them in relation to such matters as: the classes of persons who will be required to register; the means by, and frequency with which, registration information will be verified; the duration of registration; the time for reporting of changes in registration information; and the classes of registrants and the information about them that will be included on public sex offender websites.

Some commenters took issue with this basic premise of the guidelines, asserting that SORNA was meant to prescribe the most as well as the least that jurisdictions may do, hence precluding jurisdictions from adopting sex offender registration and notification measures that go beyond those required by SORNA. This view is mistaken, as may be seen from the provisions of SORNA and the Adam Walsh Act, the history of the national standards for sex offender registration and notification, and the general principles regarding preemption of state regulation by federal law.

Considering first the provisions of SORNA, § 119(a) provides the current statutory basis for the National Sex Offender Registry (NSOR), a central database maintained by the FBI that compiles information from the state sex offender registries and makes it available to law enforcement agencies on a nationwide basis. Section 119(a) states specifically that "[t]he Attorney General shall maintain a national database at the Federal Bureau of Investigation for each sex offender *and any other person required to register in a jurisdiction's sex offender registry*." (Emphasis added.) Hence, the authorizing provision for NSOR contemplates expressly that NSOR's contents will not be limited to persons satisfying the SORNA § 111(1), (5)-(8) definition of "sex offender"—which defines the universe of individuals required to register under SORNA's standards—but rather also will include information concerning "other person[s]" whom jurisdictions require to register. For example, as the guidelines note, jurisdictions may choose to require registration by certain classes of persons who are non-convicts and hence outside the SORNA definition of "sex offender"—such as persons acquitted of sexually violent crimes or child molestation offenses on the ground of insanity, or persons released following civil commitment as sexually dangerous persons. SORNA § 119(a) explicitly confirms the propriety of including information on such registrants in NSOR. If, however, there had been a legislative objective to exclude all such persons from any requirement to register, as these commenters suppose, it would have been perverse for SORNA to provide that these persons are to be included in the National Sex Offender Registry.

SORNA § 120, which provides the statutory basis for the Dru Sjodin National Sex Offender Public Website, similarly shows that SORNA was not intended to prescribe the maximum that jurisdictions may do. The website in question, maintained by the Department of Justice at www.nsopr.gov, is a search mechanism that provides convenient access through a single national site to the information available on the individual jurisdictions' public sex offender websites. Section 120(b) states that "[t]he Website shall include relevant information for each sex offender *and other person* listed on a jurisdiction's Internet site." (Emphasis added.) Hence, the provision for the national public website expressly contemplates, and allows for the inclusion of, registrants in addition to those satisfying the SORNA definition of "sex offender," and assumes that there will be public notification concerning such registrants through website posting. On the view of the commenters who assert that the SORNA standards define a ceiling for jurisdictions' programs, SORNA establishes a federal policy against registration and notification for persons who do not satisfy the SORNA definition of "sex offender." However, if a jurisdiction violates this alleged federal policy by requiring such persons to register and posting them on its sex offender website, then the violation is to be compounded by posting them on the national sex offender website as well, as SORNA § 120 requires. There is no merit to an understanding that would impute to SORNA such contradictory objectives.

A third provision of similar import is 18 U.S.C. 4042(c) (entitled "notice of sex offender release"), which requires notice to state and local law enforcement and to state or local sex offender registration agencies concerning the release to their areas of certain federal prisoners and probationers. The persons for whom such release notice is required are those "required to register under the Sex Offender Registration and Notification Act" and in addition "any other person in a category specified by the Attorney General." 18 U.S.C. 4042(c)(1), (3), as amended by SORNA § 141(f)-(g). The "any other person" language provides the Attorney General the authority to facilitate jurisdictions' registration requirements that go beyond the SORNA minimum by affording release notice to the jurisdictions' registration authorities concerning persons who may be subject to such broader requirements, even if they are not required to register by the SORNA standards. This would make no sense if there were a federal policy against jurisdictions' registering individuals who are not required to register by SORNA.

A fourth provision of this type, appearing later in the Adam Walsh Act, is § 631, which authorizes funding to assist jurisdictions in periodic verification of the registered addresses of sex offenders. The history of this provision indicates that its purpose is to support special measures jurisdictions may adopt to ensure that sex offenders remain at their registered addresses, such as mailing to the registered address verification forms that the sex offender is required to sign and return—measures that are supplementary to in-person appearances by sex offenders, which are the only means of periodic verification of registration information that SORNA requires in its enacted form. *Compare* SORNA §§ 116, 631, *with* H.R. 3132, §§ 116, 118, 109th Cong., 1st Sess. (2005) (as passed by the House of Representatives). However, under the commenters' theory that SORNA defines the maximum sex offender registration measures jurisdictions may adopt, there would be no room for a program like that authorized in § 631 of the Adam Walsh Act to encourage additional measures promoting effective sex offender tracking and location.

The general history and formulation of SORNA also imply that jurisdictions have discretion to go beyond the minimum registration and notification measures required by SORNA. SORNA was preceded by the national standards for sex offender registration under the Jacob Wetterling Crimes Against Children and Sexually Violent Offender Registration Act (42 U.S.C. 14071), which was initially enacted in 1994.

The general approach of SORNA parallels that of the Wetterling Act. Both enactments set forth standards that address the various aspects of sex offender tracking and public notification, but they do not purport to exhaust the measures that jurisdictions may wish to adopt for these purposes, or to preempt additional regulation by jurisdictions of persons who have committed sexual offenses. The Attorney General's guidelines under the Wetterling Act consistently interpreted that Act's requirements as minimum standards that states are free to exceed. *See* 64 FR 572, 575 (1999) ("[T]he Act's standards constitute a floor for state programs, not a ceiling . . . . For example, a state may have a registration system that covers broader classes of offenders than those identified in the Act, requires address verification for registered offenders at more frequent intervals than the Act prescribes, or requires offenders to register for a longer period of time than the period specified in the Act. Exercising these options creates no problem of compliance because the Act's provisions concerning duration of registration, covered offenders, and other matters do not limit state discretion to impose more extensive or stringent requirements that encompass the Act's baseline requirements."); 62 FR 39009, 39013 (1997) (same); 61 FR 15110, 15112 (1996) (same); *see also* 70 FR 12721, 12724 (2005) (same understanding in proposed guidelines for final amendments to the Wetterling Act preceding enactment of SORNA).

Given that this understanding of the national standards under the Wetterling Act was set forth in public guidelines for over a decade prior to the enactment of the successor national standards of SORNA, the reasonable expectation at the time of SORNA's enactment was that the SORNA standards would be understood in the same way, absent a new legislative direction to the contrary. Hence, continuing the approach of the Wetterling Act, SORNA does not bar jurisdictions from adopting additional regulation of sex offenders for the protection of the public, beyond the specific measures that SORNA requires.

Under both the Wetterling Act and SORNA, the "floor, not ceiling" principle is qualified in one area. Specifically, in relation to public disclosure of information on registrants, the Wetterling Act standards required release of relevant information necessary to protect the public, but with the proviso that "the identity of a victim of an offense that requires registration under this section shall not be released." 42 U.S.C. 14071(e)(2). The exclusion of victim identity from public disclosure is carried forward in SORNA § 118(b), which specifies "mandatory exemptions" from the posting of registration information on jurisdictions' sex offender websites. Specifically, § 118(b)(1) states that a jurisdiction shall exempt from disclosure "the identity of any victim of a sex offense." In addition, reflecting that SORNA § 114 requires a broader range of registration information than had been required under the Wetterling Act standards, some of which may be inappropriate for public disclosure through website posting, SORNA § 118(b) states additional mandatory exemptions for Social Security numbers, arrests not resulting in conviction, and any other information exempted from disclosure by the Attorney General.

The statement of these limited exceptions provides further confirmation for the general principle that SORNA's aim is to define a floor, not a ceiling, for jurisdictions' sex offender registration and notification programs. Under both the Wetterling Act and SORNA, there is one area—public disclosure of registration information—in which there is an overt legislative decision that the federal law standards should impose some affirmative limitation on how far jurisdictions may go. In both the Wetterling Act and SORNA this judgment is reflected in explicit statutory provisions stating that certain information shall not be disclosed. So a model for instructing jurisdictions about what they should *not* do exists, and one would expect similar express statements of limitation had SORNA been meant to prescribe upper bounds on jurisdictions' registration measures in other areas. In SORNA, however, as in the Wetterling Act, such statements of limitation do not appear in other contexts.

The practical consequences of reinterpreting the national standards to establish a ceiling for jurisdictions' registration and notification programs must also be considered. During the period in which the Wetterling Act defined the national baseline for sex offender registration and notification, states were free to go beyond the specified minimum, as discussed above, and commonly did so. For example, the Wetterling Act standards required 10 years of registration for sex offenders generally, and lifetime registration for aggravated offenders and recidivists. *See* 42 U.S.C. 14071(b)(6). But many jurisdictions have adopted durational requirements for registration that exceed the Wetterling Act's minimum, and may also exceed the current SORNA minimum in relation to many sex offenders—such as making lifetime registration the norm in relation to registrants generally, as may be provided in some existing registration programs. Hence, taking the SORNA standards as a ceiling for such programs would require many jurisdictions to reduce or eliminate sex offender registration and notification requirements that they were free to adopt under the Wetterling Act standards and currently apply in their programs. That is not plausibly the objective of a law (SORNA) enacted with the general purpose of strengthening sex offender registration and notification in the United States.

The general principles governing federal preemption of state regulation lead to the same conclusion. SORNA's regulatory system for sex offenders involves a combination of federal and non-federal elements. In part, SORNA directly prescribes registration requirements that sex offenders must comply with, and authorizes the Attorney General to augment or further specify those requirements in certain areas. *See* §§ 113(a)-(d), 114(a), 115(a), 116. These requirements are subject to direct federal enforcement, including prosecution under 18 U.S.C. 2250 where violations occur under circumstances supporting federal jurisdiction, and prescription of compliance with the SORNA requirements as mandatory conditions of supervision for federal sex offenders under 18 U.S.C. 3563(a)(8), 3583(d). SORNA provides incentives for states and other covered jurisdictions to incorporate its registration requirements for sex offenders, and other registration and notification-related measures set out in other provisions of SORNA, into their own sex offender registration and notification programs. *See* §§ 112(a), 113(c) (second sentence), 113(e), 114(b), 117, 118, 121, 122, 124-27. The overall SORNA scheme also incorporates federal superstructure and assistance measures that support and leverage the jurisdictions' individual registration and notification programs. *See* §§ 119, 120, 122, 123, 128, 142, 144, 146. The Attorney General is authorized to issue guidelines and regulations to interpret and implement SORNA. *See* § 112(b).

The commenters who took issue with the "floor, not ceiling" principle in the proposed guidelines asserted that the registration and notification requirements set out in SORNA are meant to be exhaustive and preemptive, precluding any additional regulation of released sex offenders by (non-federal) jurisdictions for the protection of the public. But "[w]hen considering pre-emption, we start with the assumption that the historic police powers of the States were not to be superseded by the Federal Act unless that was the clear and manifest purpose of Congress." *Wisconsin Public Intervenor v. Mortier*, 501 U.S. 597, 605 (1991) (internal quotation marks omitted).

One way a "clear and manifest" preemptive purpose may be shown is through "explicit pre-emptive language." 501 U.S. at 605. But SORNA contains no explicit preemption provision, which says that states or other jurisdictions cannot adopt regulatory measures beyond those that SORNA requires. The various provisions in SORNA regarding jurisdictions' implementation of SORNA are best understood as being satisfied if a jurisdiction incorporates the SORNA requirements in its program, with no negative implication concerning the jurisdiction's discretion to adopt additional requirements. *See* SORNA §§ 112(a) (each jurisdiction to maintain a sex offender registry conforming to the requirements of SORNA), 124 (each jurisdiction to implement SORNA within specified time frames), 125 (funding reduction for jurisdictions that fail to substantially implement SORNA), 126 (authorizing funding assistance for implementation of SORNA).

Absent explicit preemption, "Congress' intent to supersede state law in a given area may nonetheless be implicit if a scheme of federal regulation is so pervasive as to make reasonable the inference that Congress left no room for the States to supplement it." 501 U.S. at 605 (internal quotation marks omitted). SORNA, however, obviously leaves room for states (and other jurisdictions) to supplement its requirements. As discussed above, this point is recognized in provisions of SORNA relating to its federal superstructure elements, such as the National Sex Offender Registry and the Dru Sjodin National Sex Offender Website, which expressly presuppose that the jurisdictions' programs may go beyond the SORNA-required minimum.

Preemption may also be inferred if "the Act of Congress . . . touch[es] a field in which the federal interest is so dominant that the federal system will be assumed to preclude enforcement of state laws on the same subject." 501 U.S. at 605 (internal quotation marks omitted). There is, however, no such predominant federal interest with respect to sex offender registration and notification. The interest of the individual states (and other covered jurisdictions) in the protection of their people from sex offenders through appropriate regulatory measures and public disclosure of relevant information is at least equal to that of the federal government, and falls within an area of traditional state power and responsibility.

71

Another ground for inferring preemption is "if the goals sought to be obtained and the obligations imposed reveal a purpose to preclude state authority." 501 U.S. at 605 (internal quotation marks omitted). Here as well, SORNA does not support such an inference. The general purpose of SORNA is "to protect the public from sex offenders and offenders against children," and to that end Congress in SORNA "establish[ed] a comprehensive national system for the registration of those offenders." SORNA § 102. The SORNA requirements are "comprehensive" in the sense that SORNA provides a full set of national baseline requirements and procedures for sex offender registration and notification, replacing the previous national standards under the Wetterling Act. *See* SORNA § 129 (repeal of Wetterling Act upon completion of implementation period for SORNA). Moreover, SORNA is more comprehensive and contemplates greater uniformity among jurisdictions than the previous Wetterling Act standards in that it generally establishes a higher national baseline. But the "comprehensive[ness]" of the SORNA requirements cannot be understood to reflect an intent to preclude any and all differences among jurisdictions. Some provisions in SORNA expressly authorize variations among jurisdictions. *See* §§ 118(c) (discretionary exemption of certain information from website posting by jurisdictions), 125(b) (authorizing accommodation of state constitutional restrictions). Various other SORNA provisions, as discussed above, recognize that jurisdictions may go beyond the SORNA minimum and they provide for the accommodation of such differences in SORNA's federal superstructure elements, including the National Sex Offender Registry and the Dru Sjodin National Sex Offender Website. These express provisions are at odds with any understanding of the "comprehensive[ness]" of the SORNA standards in a preemptive sense, so as to preclude the adoption by states or other covered jurisdictions of measures that seek to go further in order to advance SORNA's basic purpose, i.e., "[i]n order to protect the public from sex offenders and offenders against children." SORNA § 102.

Finally, "[e]ven when Congress has not chosen to occupy a particular field, pre-emption may occur to the extent that state and federal law actually conflict." 501 U.S. at 605. The comments received on the proposed guidelines included one argument along these lines, relating specifically to the provisions in SORNA § 115 concerning the duration of registration.

By way of background, subsection (a) of § 115 requires a sex offender to register "for the full registration period . . . unless the offender is allowed a reduction under subsection (b)." The "full registration period[s]" specified in subsection (a) of § 115 are 15 years for tier I sex offenders, 25 years for tier II sex offenders, and life for tier III sex offenders. Subsection (b) of § 115 in turn provides that the full registration period required by federal law shall be reduced for certain sex offenders who maintain a "clean record" as defined in the statute. Specifically, the "full registration period" specified for tier I sex offenders in subsection (a)(1) is 15 years, but if the sex offender maintains a clean record for 10 years, subsection (b) reduces by five years the period for which subsection (a) would otherwise require such a sex offender to register. The other "clean record" reduction of the registration period required by federal law under § 115(b) is for tier III sex offenders registered on the basis of juvenile delinquency adjudications who maintain a clean record for 25 years; no reduction is authorized for tier II sex offenders or for tier III sex offenders registered on the basis of adult convictions.

One of the commenters argued that these provisions presuppose that the "full registration period[s]" specified in § 115(a) are the longest registration periods SORNA allows jurisdictions to impose on sex offenders. For if a jurisdiction required lifetime registration for a tier I sex offender, the five-year reduction of the full registration period § 115(b) requires in case the sex offender maintains a "clean record" for 10 years could not meaningfully be applied.

However, in the context of § 115, the federal registration periods described in subsection (a) are referred to as the "full" registration periods to distinguish such periods from the reduced federal registration periods required under subsection (b) if certain "clean record" conditions are satisfied. There is no basis for taking subsection (a)'s requirement that sex offenders register for the periods specified in that subsection as implying that jurisdictions cannot prescribe longer or additional registration requirements for sex offenders. Subsection (b) of § 115 provides that the period for which SORNA requires a sex offender to register shall be reduced upon satisfaction of the "clean record" conditions specified in that subsection, but no inference follows that states (or other jurisdictions) lack the discretion to require on their own authority that sex offenders continue to register beyond the periods that SORNA requires them to register.

Hence, a jurisdiction has not failed to implement the SORNA requirements if it terminates registration for tier I sex offenders after they have maintained "clean records" for 10 years, as § 115(b) allows. But if a jurisdiction chooses instead to require longer periods of registration for such offenders, including lifetime registration, it has done nothing that SORNA prohibits. As with SORNA's requirements generally, § 115's durational requirements for registration define the minimum, and not the maximum, requirements for the jurisdictions' registration programs.

Accordingly, no change has been made in the final guidelines as to the general principle that SORNA defines a floor, not a ceiling, for jurisdictions' sex offender registration and notification programs. Changes in the final guidelines relating to this issue are limited to edits in Parts II.B and XII for greater clarity on the points reflected in the foregoing discussion.

C. Retroactivity

The proposed guidelines require the application by a jurisdiction of SORNA's requirements to sex offenders convicted prior to the enactment of SORNA or its implementation in the jurisdiction, if they remain in the system as prisoners, supervisees, or registrants, or if they reenter the system because of subsequent criminal convictions. Some commenters objected to this feature of the proposed guidelines as adversely affecting sex offenders in these classes. However, the effects of SORNA's registration and notification requirements on sex offenders are much the same regardless of whether their sex offense convictions occurred before or after SORNA's enactment or its implementation in a particular jurisdiction. Likewise, the public safety concerns presented by sex offenders are much the same, regardless of when they were convicted. The SORNA standards reflect a legislative judgment that SORNA's registration and notification requirements, even if disagreeable from the standpoint of sex offenders who are subject to them, are justified by the resulting benefits in promoting public safety. The comments received do not establish that this legislative judgment is wrong, and in any event such a premise could not be accepted in the formulation of guidelines whose objective is to "interpret and implement" SORNA's standards, *see* SORNA § 112(b), not to second-guess the legislative policies they embody.

Moreover, the specific provisions of the guidelines relating to "retroactivity" incorporate some features that may limit their effect on sex offenders with older convictions. While SORNA's requirements apply to all sex offenders, regardless of when they were convicted, *see* 28 CFR 72.3, the guidelines do not require jurisdictions to identify and register every such sex offender. Rather, as stated in the guidelines, a jurisdiction will be considered to have substantially implemented SORNA if it applies SORNA's requirements to sex offenders who remain in the system as prisoners, supervisees, or registrants, or reenter the system through subsequent convictions. So the guidelines do not require a jurisdiction to register in conformity with SORNA sex offenders who have fully left the system and merged into the general population at the time the jurisdiction implements SORNA, if they do not reoffend. A further limitation permitted by the guidelines is that a jurisdiction may credit a sex offender with a pre-SORNA conviction with the time elapsed from his release (or the time elapsed from sentencing, in case of a nonincarcerative sentence) in determining what, if any, remaining registration time is required. To the extent that a jurisdiction exercises this option, the effect of retroactive application on sex offenders with pre-SORNA convictions may be further reduced.

Where the critical comments about the guidelines' treatment of retroactivity went beyond considerations that fail to distinguish sex offenders with pre-SORNA (or pre-SORNA-implementation) convictions from those with more recent convictions, they tended to argue that retroactive application of SORNA's requirements would be unconstitutional, or would be unfair to sex offenders who could not have anticipated the resulting applicability of SORNA's requirements at the time of their entry of a guilty plea to the predicate sex offense. However, as non-punitive regulatory measures, the SORNA requirements do not implicate the Constitution's prohibition of ex post facto laws. Moreover, fairness does not require that an offender, at the time he acknowledges his commission of the crime and pleads guilty, be able to anticipate all future regulatory measures that may be adopted in relation to persons like him for public safety purposes. The comments received provided no persuasive distinction on these points between the SORNA requirements and the sex offender registration and notification measures upheld by the Supreme Court against an ex post facto challenge in *Smith v. Doe*, 538 U.S. 84 (2003).

For the foregoing reasons, no changes have been made in the final guidelines relating to retroactivity based on the comments alleging an adverse effect on sex offenders. Some critical comments were also received relating to the guidelines' treatment of retroactivity based on potential practical difficulties for jurisdictions in identifying offenders in the relevant classes and determining what SORNA requires in relation to them. These comments are discussed below in connection with Part IX of the guidelines.

D. Automation – Electronic Databases and Software

Some commenters asked for a more extensive set of technological or documentary tools to facilitate the implementation of SORNA in their jurisdictions. The SMART Office is developing, and will make available to jurisdictions, a wide range of tools of this type. Descriptions of many of them appear in the initial portion of this summary, under the caption "aids to implementation."

E. Implementation

The final guidelines, like the proposed guidelines, explain the "substantial implementation" standard for jurisdictions' implementation of the SORNA requirements as affording a limited latitude to approve measures that do not exactly follow the provisions of SORNA or the guidelines, where the departure from a SORNA requirement does not substantially disserve the requirement's objective. Some commenters urged that a much broader understanding of the "substantial implementation" standard should be adopted, under which a jurisdiction's registration and notification system could be approved even if the jurisdiction made no effort to do (either exactly or approximately) what SORNA requires according to its terms, but rather adopted a fundamentally different approach to sex offender registration and notification generally or to particular registration or notification requirements.

In practical terms, this understanding of "substantial implementation" would potentially negate all of the particular legislative judgments in SORNA concerning sex offender registration and notification requirements. It would effectively treat them as a set of suggestions for furthering public safety in relation to released sex offenders, which could be dispensed with based on arguments that other approaches would further that general objective, though not encompassing the specific minimum measures that SORNA prescribes or anything close to those measures.

This reinterpretation of the substantial implementation standard has not been adopted in the final guidelines because it would defeat SORNA's objective of establishing a national baseline for sex offender registration and notification. Section 125 of SORNA illuminates this point. Subsection (a) of that section requires a reduction of Byrne Grant funding to jurisdictions that fail to "substantially implement this title [i.e., SORNA]" within the applicable time frame. Subsection (b) of the section recognizes, however, that there may be some instances in which a jurisdiction cannot substantially implement SORNA "because of a demonstrated inability to implement certain provisions that would place a jurisdiction in violation of its constitution, as determined by a ruling of the jurisdiction's highest court." In such circumstances, the section provides that the Attorney General and the jurisdiction are to consult to verify that there is an actual conflict between the state constitution and SORNA's requirements and to determine whether any such conflict can be reconciled. If there proves to be an irreconcilable conflict, then special provision is made for such situations, as provided in § 125(b)(3): "If the jurisdiction is unable to substantially implement this title because of a limitation imposed by the jurisdiction's constitution, the Attorney General may determine that the jurisdiction is in compliance with this Act if the jurisdiction has made, or is in the process of implementing reasonable alternative procedures or accommodations, which are consistent with the purposes of this Act."

Hence, § 125 distinguishes between two standards for approval of a jurisdiction's SORNA implementation efforts: (i) the generally applicable standard of "substantial implementation," and (ii) a more permissive standard allowing reasonable alternative procedures or accommodations that are consistent with SORNA's purposes. The latter (more permissive) standard is applicable only to the extent that there is an irreconcilable conflict between substantial implementation of SORNA's requirements and what the jurisdiction's constitution allows.

The commenters who have urged an open-ended understanding of the "substantial implementation" standard would collapse the distinction drawn by § 125 between substantial implementation on the one hand and, on the other, alternative measures that do not substantially implement SORNA's requirements but aim to further its purposes in some more general way. Under § 125, the latter are allowed only if state constitutional restrictions preclude doing substantially what SORNA requires according to its terms. But under these commenters' view, alternative measures could be allowed without any particular limitation, even where a jurisdiction's constitution creates no impediment to doing what SORNA's provisions prescribe. Given the clear distinction that § 125 draws between substantial implementation of SORNA and adoption of alternative measures that are consistent with SORNA's purposes (but do not substantially implement SORNA), the commenters' view on this point cannot be reconciled with SORNA.

This point can be illustrated concretely by considering specific alternatives that some commenters have proposed. For example, some commenters have urged that "risk-based" approaches to sex offender registration and notification—i.e., systems in which registration or notification requirements are premised on individualized risk assessments of offenders—should be approved as substantially implementing SORNA.

The terminology utilized by the commenters on this point—distinguishing systems that incorporate SORNA's requirements from "risk-based" systems—is misleading, in that SORNA gives weight to various factors that are reasonably related to the risk that sex offenders may pose to others and the need for protective measures. Not all persons who have committed offenses of a sexual nature are required to register under SORNA's standards, but only those convicted for "sex offenses" as defined in SORNA § 111(5). The definition incorporates a number of limitations, including general exclusions of offenses involving consensual sexual conduct between adults, and of offenses involving consensual sexual conduct with minors at least 13 years old where the offender is not more than four years older. Within the universe of sex offenders who are required to register under the SORNA standards, SORNA does not prescribe registration and notification requirements indiscriminately. Rather, SORNA varies the required duration of registration, the frequency of required in-person appearances for verification, and required public notification through website posting, based on "tier" criteria that take account of such factors as the nature and seriousness of the offense, the age of the victim, and the extent of the offender's recidivism. *See* SORNA § 111(2)-(4), 115-16, 118(c)(1). SORNA also reduces the periods for which it requires sex offenders to register in certain circumstances based on criteria relating to the offender's subsequent conduct, including avoidance of further offending, successful completion of supervision, and successful completion of treatment. *See* SORNA § 115(b)(1). Moreover, given that SORNA generally defines a floor rather than a ceiling for jurisdictions' registration and notification programs, there is no inconsistency with SORNA if a jurisdiction carries out risk assessments of offenders that take into account a broader range of factors, and prescribes registration or notification requirements beyond the SORNA minimum requirements based on the results of such assessments.

These commenters' recommendation, however, is that systems should be approved as substantially implementing SORNA that do not incorporate the SORNA minimum requirements, but rather prescribe lesser registration or notification requirements (or no requirements) for sex offenders, unless they are deemed to meet some threshold or level of risk based on risk assessments that take account of factors beyond those allowed under SORNA's provisions. The grounds offered in support of this recommendation are that such systems arguably offer various benefits in comparison with SORNA's standards, such as focusing registration and notification more effectively on the offenders who are likely to pose the greatest risk to the public, and providing registrants with an incentive to follow the rules and improve their behavior, where doing so may reduce their risk scores and hence result in a reduction or termination of registration or notification.

This recommendation cannot be accepted because the systems described by such commenters do not substantially implement the SORNA requirements, and do not attempt to do so. Rather, they propose to forego implementation of what SORNA does require in favor of pursuing different approaches that the commenters view as preferable means of promoting public safety from sex offenders.

There is one circumstance in which SORNA allows the approval of such alternative measures to be considered. Suppose that the highest court of a jurisdiction rules that the jurisdiction's constitution does not permit certain registration or notification measures required by SORNA to be taken in relation to a sex offender, unless the offender is found to satisfy some threshold or level of risk based on a risk assessment that gives weight to factors that SORNA's specific provisions do not allow as grounds for waiving or reducing registration or notification requirements. In the presence of such an irreconcilable conflict with the jurisdiction's constitution, the Attorney General would be permitted under SORNA § 125(b)(3) to approve the jurisdiction's adoption of reasonable alternative procedures that are consistent with SORNA's purposes, but that incorporate reliance on risk assessments and depart from compliance with SORNA's specific requirements to the extent necessitated by the conflict. However, the commenters' recommendation is that systems going below the SORNA-required minima based on risk assessments should be allowed as "substantial implementation" of SORNA even where implementing SORNA according to its terms would not conflict with the jurisdiction's constitution. This recommendation cannot be accepted because it is inconsistent with the distinction that § 125 draws between substantial implementation of SORNA and reasonable alternative measures that do not substantially implement SORNA but are consistent with SORNA's purposes. Understanding "substantial implementation" so broadly would potentially reduce SORNA's specific standards to mere advice, and would conflict with the provisions in § 125 that specially authorize a more permissive standard only under narrowly defined circumstances involving constitutional conflicts.

The response is essentially the same to other specific alternatives that some commenters have urged as "substantially implementing" SORNA, such as not requiring registration by juveniles adjudicated delinquent for sex offenses under any circumstances, or making registration or notification for such delinquents a matter of judicial discretion. SORNA § 111(8) incorporates considered legislative judgments concerning the class of juvenile delinquency adjudications that are to be treated as "convictions" for purposes of SORNA's registration and notification requirements, a point that is discussed in greater detail below in connection with Part IV.A of the guidelines. The effect of the § 111(8) definition is that the application of SORNA's registration and notification requirements to juvenile delinquents is generally limited to those who are at least 14 years old and who are adjudicated delinquent for the most serious sexually assaultive crimes. In addition, SORNA § 115(b)(3)(B) allows the registration periods for persons required to register based on juvenile delinquency adjudications to be reduced in certain circumstances, based on their subsequent good behavior, where no corresponding reduction is allowed for offenders required to register based on adult convictions.

These commenters' proposal is in effect that a jurisdiction should be deemed to have substantially implemented SORNA with respect to the treatment of juveniles adjudicated delinquent for sex offenses if it ignores what SORNA provides on this issue, and instead does something different that the commenters believe to be better policy. As with the earlier example of "risk assessment" systems, there are circumstances under which SORNA would allow alternative approaches with respect to juvenile delinquents to be considered. Suppose, for example, that the highest court of a jurisdiction holds that the jurisdiction's constitution does not permit categorical registration or notification requirements for juvenile delinquents—even for the narrowly defined class of juveniles adjudicated delinquent for the most serious sexually assaultive crimes, as described in SORNA § 111(8). Rather, the court holds that the jurisdiction's constitution requires that such measures be contingent on judicial determinations that registration or notification is appropriate for particular juveniles. In the presence of such an irreconcilable conflict with the jurisdiction's constitution, the Attorney General would be permitted under SORNA § 125(b)(3) to approve the jurisdiction's adoption of reasonable alternative procedures that are consistent with SORNA's purposes, but that depart from compliance with SORNA's requirements regarding juveniles to the extent necessitated by the conflict. However, the commenters' proposal is that the same latitude should be afforded as "substantial implementation" of SORNA even where there is no conflict with the jurisdiction's constitution in implementing SORNA's provisions regarding juveniles according to their terms. This is not consistent with SORNA for the reasons discussed above.

For the foregoing reasons, no change has been made in the final guidelines as to the basic understanding of the substantial implementation standard. There is some limited modification in the final guidelines' explanation of this standard for greater clarity concerning the points noted in the discussion above.

III.   Covered Jurisdictions

The comments received did not show a need to change the guidelines' explanation concerning the "jurisdictions" that are subject to SORNA's requirements, except with respect to the treatment of Indian tribes.

Section 127 of SORNA provides the standards that determine whether an Indian tribe is a registration jurisdiction for purposes of SORNA. Section 127 generally afforded tribes an election between carrying out the SORNA requirements as jurisdictions subject to its provisions, or electing to delegate the SORNA registration and notification functions to the states within which the tribes are located. The period for such elections by tribes under § 127 ended on July 27, 2007. Within that period, close to 200 tribes—the vast majority of those eligible to make an election under § 127—elected to be SORNA registration jurisdictions. Tribes that have made this election are not required to duplicate sex offender registration and notification functions that are carried out by the states in which they are located, and are free to enter into agreements with such states for the shared or cooperative discharge of these functions, as provided in § 127(b). The discussion of § 127 in the guidelines has been updated to reflect the expiration of the period for tribal elections under that provision.

As noted at the start of this summary, there are also substantive changes in the final guidelines that have been adopted on the basis of comments received from groups or associations of tribes, individual tribes, or their representatives, relating to the status or treatment of Indian tribes as SORNA jurisdictions or associated consequences. These include some changes of broad effect.

The final guidelines provide that tribes may enter into cooperative arrangements among themselves to effect the substantial implementation of the SORNA requirements. For example, a group of tribes with adjacent territories may find it helpful to enter into an agreement under which the participating tribes contribute resources and information to the extent of their capacities, but the tribal police department (or some other agency) of one of the tribes in the group has primary responsibility for the direct discharge of the various functions required for registration of sex offenders subject to the jurisdiction of any of the tribes in the group. Under such an arrangement, the responsible agency in the selected tribe might generally handle initially registering sex offenders who enter the jurisdiction of any of the tribes in the group, receiving information from those sex offenders concerning subsequent changes in residence or other registration information, and conducting periodic in-person appearances by the registrants to verify and update the registration information, as SORNA requires. Likewise, with respect to maintenance of websites providing public access to sex offender information, as required by SORNA § 118, one option for a tribe—explicitly authorized by SORNA § 127(b)(2)—would be to adopt a cooperative agreement with a state in which it is located to include information concerning the sex offenders subject to the tribe's jurisdiction on the state's sex offender website. But an additional option afforded under the final guidelines is for tribes to enter into agreements or arrangements among themselves for the shared administration or operation of websites covering the sex offenders of the participating tribes.

Although SORNA does not explicitly authorize intertribal agreements or arrangements for the cooperative discharge of registration and notification functions, there is no inconsistency

79

between appropriately designed arrangements of this type and realization of SORNA's substantive objectives for sex offender registration and notification. Moreover, such arrangements may facilitate tribal implementation of SORNA by allowing the pooling of resources and expertise and avoiding the need for duplication of effort among tribes with similar registration and notification responsibilities. The implementation of the SORNA requirements by tribes through such cooperative arrangements with other tribes will accordingly be considered as satisfying the SORNA substantial implementation standard.

Beyond concerns about facilitating cooperative intertribal efforts, which are addressed in the final guidelines as discussed above, a common theme in the comments received from tribes or tribal organizations was concern about the treatment of tribes that are not registration jurisdictions for SORNA purposes. Some commenters urged that tribes subject to state law enforcement jurisdiction under 18 U.S.C. 1162 be treated more like tribes that are allowed to be SORNA registration jurisdictions under SORNA § 127 and have made elections to that effect. SORNA § 127(a)(2)(A) provides that the SORNA registration and notification functions for tribes within the scope of 18 U.S.C. 1162 are automatically delegated to the state. As this is a statutory matter, the guidelines cannot change it.

However, the final guidelines have been modified to make it clear that § 1162 tribes are not excluded from carrying out sex offender registration and notification functions, either as an exercise of their sovereign powers to the extent that there is no conflict with the state's discharge of its responsibilities under SORNA, or pursuant to a decision by the state that sex offender registration functions can be most effectively carried out by tribal authorities with respect to sex offenders subject to the tribe's jurisdiction. Moreover, states have the same responsibility to carry out the SORNA registration and notification functions in relation to sex offenders in § 1162 tribal areas as they do in relation to sex offenders in other areas in the state. The SMART Office will take seriously the need to ensure that all states within the scope of § 1162 discharge these responsibilities. The same points apply in relation to the relatively small number of tribes that were eligible to make an election to be a SORNA registration jurisdiction under the terms of SORNA § 127(a)(1)(A) but have not made such an election.

Some commenters expressed more specific concerns about ensuring that tribes that are not SORNA registration jurisdictions receive notice concerning the entry or presence of sex offenders in their territories. In this connection, the notification requirements of SORNA § 121 apply in relation to all entities within a state as described in that section. This will serve to make information concerning the location and relocation of sex offenders available to agencies, organizations, and individuals in tribes that are not SORNA registration jurisdictions, as with others agencies and organizations within the state. Specific requirements and means of access to such information under § 121(b) are discussed in Part VII.B of the guidelines.

A number of tribal commenters expressed concerns about SORNA § 127(a)(2)(C), which provides for delegation of the SORNA registration and notification functions to the state or states within which a tribe is located if "the Attorney General determines that the tribe has not substantially implemented the requirements of this subtitle and is not likely to become capable of doing so within a reasonable amount of time." This provision for involuntary delegation to a state or states in the specified circumstances was included in SORNA to foreclose any possibility of uncloseable gaps in the nationwide network of sex offender registration and notification programs. The Department of Justice hopes and expects, however, that the occurrence of such an involuntary delegation will never be necessary, given the strong interest of the tribes in effective registration and notification for sex offenders subject to their jurisdictions, and the priority that the SMART Office gives to working with all tribes and other jurisdictions to facilitate the implementation of SORNA's requirements in relation to tribal areas. Moreover, substantial time remains for tribal implementation efforts. Tribal jurisdictions, like other jurisdictions, enjoy the three-year grace period provided by SORNA § 124 for SORNA implementation (commencing on July 27, 2006), and the possibility of an extension of time for up to an additional two years under that provision. In addition, § 127(a)(2)(C) does not require an involuntary delegation if a tribe fails to implement SORNA within the normally allowed time under § 124, unless the Attorney General makes a further determination that the tribe is not likely to become capable of substantially implementing SORNA within a reasonable amount of time.

IV.   Covered Sex Offenses and Sex Offenders

A. Convictions Generally

Tribal Convictions

The proposed guidelines stated that jurisdictions could choose not to require registration based on Indian tribal sex offense convictions, where the defendant had not been afforded a right to counsel to which he would have been entitled in comparable state proceedings. Many comments received from tribal organizations and individual tribes objected to this provision. They argued that tribal convictions should be respected, and noted that many procedural protections for defendants are provided in tribal proceedings as a matter of federal law and in practice, including the right to counsel (though defined differently from the corresponding right in state proceedings). *See* 25 U.S.C. 1302.

These comments are persuasive. SORNA's registration and notification requirements are premised on a person's conviction for a sex offense. *See, e.g.*, SORNA §§ 111(1), 113(a). With respect to covered "sex offense[s]," SORNA provides no basis for differentiating between tribal offenses and offenses under the laws of other domestic jurisdictions. Rather, it states expressly that "sex offense" includes "criminal offense[s]" of specified types, and that "criminal offense" in the relevant sense means "a State, local, *tribal*, foreign, or military offense . . . or other criminal offense." SORNA § 111(5)(A)(i)-(ii), 111(6) (emphasis added).

Likewise, with respect to "conviction[s]," SORNA does not differentiate between tribal convictions and convictions by other U.S. jurisdictions. SORNA does incorporate a special proviso with respect to foreign convictions, stating in § 111(5)(B) that "[a] foreign conviction is not a sex offense for the purposes of this title if it was not obtained with sufficient safeguards for fundamental fairness and due process for the accused under guidelines or regulations established under section 112." If it had similarly been contemplated that the Attorney General's guidelines would adopt further conditions for the effectiveness of Indian tribal convictions under SORNA, one would have expected SORNA to include some proviso comparable to § 111(5)(B) for tribal convictions. But SORNA contains no such proviso.

The final guidelines accordingly do not differentiate between tribal convictions and convictions by other United States jurisdictions as predicates for sex offender registration and notification.

Nominal Variations on "Conviction"

The proposed guidelines stated that SORNA's requirements are not waived by nominal or terminological variations in the designations that jurisdictions use in referring to the dispositions of criminal cases. For example, SORNA's requirements remain applicable if a jurisdiction has a procedure under which certain sex offense convictions (e.g., those of young adult sex offenders who satisfy certain criteria) are referred to as something other than "convictions," or are nominally "vacated" or "set aside," but the sex offender remains subject to penal consequences based on the conviction. Some commenters objected to this aspect of the proposed guidelines, arguing that jurisdictions should be free to make SORNA's requirements inapplicable by such means.

The issue raised by these comments is whether individual jurisdictions have a free hand to stipulate that the dispositions of criminal cases do not constitute "convictions" for purposes of SORNA. If that were the case, a jurisdiction could make the SORNA registration and notification requirements inapplicable to its sex offenders merely by varying its terminology—referring to certain classes of criminal convictions for sex offenses by some term other than "conviction"—and there would then be no national baseline of covered sex offenders and registration/notification requirements applicable thereto.

Such an approach would be inconsistent with SORNA's purpose to establish "a comprehensive national system for the registration of [sex] offenders." SORNA § 102. SORNA's requirements apply to anyone who "was convicted of a sex offense." *See* SORNA §§ 111(1) (defining "sex offender"), 113 (applying SORNA's registration requirements to "sex offender[s]"). While the statutory definitions of sex offenses falling within SORNA's registration categories, *see* SORNA § 111(5)-(8), will vary from jurisdiction to jurisdiction, the meaning of "convicted" for purposes of SORNA is a matter of federal law, and its applicability is not determined by the terminology a jurisdiction uses in referring to the disposition of a criminal case. Notably, in light of SORNA § 111(8), even certain juvenile delinquents are deemed to be "convicted" and hence required to register under SORNA's standards, if the juvenile is at least 14 years old and the offense for which the juvenile was adjudicated delinquent is sufficiently serious. But under these commenters' proposal, jurisdictions could avoid requiring registration for an *adult* offender convicted of such a crime merely by using some other term in referring to the conviction (e.g., "youthful offender disposition").

SORNA does not afford such latitude to waive its requirements in this manner and no change has been made in the final guidelines on this point.

Juvenile Adjudications

A number of commenters criticized the proposed guidelines' explanation of SORNA § 111(8), which provides that certain juvenile delinquency adjudications are to be treated as convictions for registration purposes under SORNA. Many of these commenters argued that registration or public notification concerning juveniles adjudicated delinquent for sex offenses would be inappropriate or counterproductive, on such grounds as the following: that juveniles are less likely to reoffend, less culpable, and more amenable to treatment than adult offenders; that registration of juveniles will deter reporting of their crimes by their families and will promote avoidance of adjudicatory dispositions of their cases that reflect the actual offense conduct; that juveniles subject to registration or notification will be adversely affected with respect to education, employment, treatment, socialization, and personal security; and that premising registration or notification on juvenile delinquency adjudications is at odds with the characteristics and objectives of juvenile justice systems, including their requirements of confidentiality and orientation towards treatment and rehabilitation. The commenters advanced various recommendations for addressing these concerns, including not registering juveniles at all, making registration or notification for juveniles a matter of judicial discretion, or limiting registration or notification for juveniles to cases involving particularly violent or serious sex offenses.

The more far reaching proposals for changes concerning the treatment of juveniles cannot be accepted because they would require a nullification of the judgment in SORNA that a narrowly defined class of juvenile delinquency adjudications are to be treated on a par with adult convictions for registration and notification purposes. Predecessor bills to SORNA took divergent approaches to this issue. Some excluded juvenile delinquents entirely from their registration and notification requirements, while others provided that juvenile delinquency adjudications would be treated the same as adult convictions across the board. *Compare* S. 1086, §§ 102(1), 110, 109th Cong., 2d Sess. (2006) (exclusion of juvenile delinquency adjudications in Senate-passed bill), *with* H.R. 3132, § 111(3), 109th Cong., 1st Sess. (2005) (juvenile delinquency adjudications treated the same as adult convictions in House-passed bill).

The resolution of this issue in SORNA as enacted is an intermediate approach that does not generally require that juveniles be treated the same as adults, but does affirmatively treat certain juvenile delinquency adjudications as "convictions," and the juveniles subject to such adjudications as "sex offenders" subject to the SORNA registration and notification requirements, under the following criteria: (i) the juvenile must have been at least 14 years old at the time of the offense, (ii) the offense adjudicated was comparable to or more severe than aggravated sexual abuse (as described in 18 U.S.C. 2241) or an attempt or conspiracy to commit such an offense, and (iii) the registration period to which the juvenile is subject may be reduced from life to 25 years if certain "clean record" conditions are satisfied. *See* SORNA §§ 111(1), (8), 115(b)(3)(B). This is the legislative decision that the guidelines must "interpret and implement." SORNA § 112(b). There is no authority to abrogate it or to approve some basically different system for registering (or not registering) juveniles adjudicated delinquent for sex offenses.

As noted above, a more moderate recommendation advanced by some of the commenters was that registration or notification for juveniles be limited to cases involving particularly violent or serious sex offenses. This is more in line with what SORNA actually does provide, limiting the predicate offenses for registration based on juvenile delinquency adjudications to those "comparable to" aggravated sexual abuse as described in 18 U.S.C. 2241 (or an attempt or conspiracy to commit such an offense).

It was noted in the comments, however, that under the interpretation of this standard in the proposed guidelines, it could potentially reach some cases not involving sex offenses of the most serious nature, such as a case involving a juvenile delinquency adjudication of a 14-year-old for engaging in consensual sexual play with an 11-year-old. A number of commenters questioned the suitability of such juvenile adjudications as the basis for lengthy or lifetime registration and public notification, and indicated that an inflexible application of the SORNA juvenile coverage requirement to reach such cases could constitute a substantial impediment to jurisdictions' implementation of SORNA.

These comments have provided grounds for further thought concerning the measures that will be considered substantial implementation of SORNA in relation to juveniles adjudicated delinquent for sex offenses. The federal offense of aggravated sexual abuse, 18 U.S.C. 2241, which provides the touchstone for juvenile coverage under SORNA § 111(8), encompasses a range of serious sexually assaultive conduct that would correspond roughly to the common understanding of the notion of "rape." Specifically, it proscribes engaging in a sexual act with another by means of force or the threat of serious violence, or by rendering unconscious or involuntarily drugging the victim. These aspects of the offense apply regardless of the age of the perpetrator or victim.

However, there are certain features of 18 U.S.C. 2241 that provide a broader compass in cases involving victims who fall below specified age thresholds. Specifically, sexual acts with victims below the age of 12 are covered, even in cases involving no overt violence or coercion. *See* 18 U.S.C. 2241(c). In addition, under the associated definition of covered "sexual act[s]," the relevant acts are for the most part those involving penetration, but direct genital touching—which would otherwise support only liability for lesser "sexual contact" offenses—is treated as a covered "sexual act" if the victim is below the age of 16. *See* 18 U.S.C. 2246(2)(D).

In relation to the aspects of 18 U.S.C. 2241 that depend specially on the age of the victim, there is no difficulty in applying them without qualification as a basis for sex offender registration and notification in cases involving adult offenders. For example, a 30-year-old who engages in sexual activity with an 11-year-old plausibly falls within a class of persons who may constitute a danger to children, and the protective functions served by SORNA's registration and notification requirements are implicated, regardless of finer issues concerning the victim's acquiescence or resistance or the exact nature of the sexual activity.

In comparison, SORNA's public safety objectives may not be similarly implicated by juvenile cases like those pointed to by the commenters, such as a case involving a 14-year-old adjudicated delinquent based on consensual sexual play with an 11-year-old. Cases of this type

84

fall within the definitional scope of 18 U.S.C. 2241 only because of special features of that provision that create liability for nonviolent or lesser sexual offenses based on the victim's age. But in such a case, the delinquent may himself be a child who is not far removed in age from the victim, and the offense may be one that would not entail comparable registration and notification requirements for an adult offender, if committed by the adult offender against a victim who was near in age to himself.

Based on this reconsideration of the juvenile coverage issue, the final guidelines reflect a judgment that the objectives of SORNA § 111(8) will not be substantially undermined if jurisdictions are afforded discretion concerning registration and notification for juveniles adjudicated delinquent on the basis of offenses that are within the definitional scope of 18 U.S.C. 2241 only because of the age of the victim. In positive terms, jurisdictions will be considered to have substantially implemented SORNA in this context if they apply SORNA's registration and notification requirements to juveniles at least 14 years old who are adjudicated delinquent for committing offenses amounting to rape or its equivalent (or an attempt or conspiracy to commit such an offense), as specified in the final guidelines.

B. Foreign Convictions

Some commenters expressed the concern that the requirement under SORNA to register sex offenders based on foreign convictions would create unmanageable burdens on jurisdictions to assess the fairness of foreign judicial proceedings. However, the guidelines have been formulated so as to minimize any such burden. In part, they require registration categorically based on sex offense convictions under the laws of four specified foreign countries—Canada, United Kingdom, Australia, and New Zealand—and based on convictions in countries whose judicial systems have been favorably assessed in the Country Reports on Human Rights Practices that are prepared by the U.S. Department of State. Jurisdictions are not required to exempt any sex offense convictions in other foreign countries from registration requirements, but if they wish to do so, they may exempt convictions that they consider unreliable indicia of factual guilt, utilizing whatever process or procedure they choose to adopt in making such determinations. The treatment of foreign convictions has accordingly not been changed in the final guidelines, except for limited editing to emphasize the extent of jurisdictions' discretion in approaching this issue, and correcting a reference to "Great Britain" in the proposed guidelines to refer instead to "United Kingdom."

C.-E. Sex Offenses Generally; Specified Offenses Against Minors; Protected Witnesses

The proposed guidelines' general explanation of SORNA's offense coverage requirements and exceptions or qualifications relating to protected witnesses have not been substantially changed in the final guidelines. Critical comments relating to this aspect of the guidelines largely reflected misapprehensions that SORNA requires registration based on offenses that are not in the SORNA registration categories—e.g., consensual sexual offenses involving minors or youth of like age—or proposed changes that SORNA does not allow, such as waiving registration based on offenses in the covered categories unless the offender is found to meet some threshold of likely dangerousness under a "risk assessment" system.

V.   Classes of Sex Offenders

The proposed guidelines' general explanation of SORNA's "tiers," and their implications for registration and notification requirements, have not been substantially changed in the final guidelines. The critical comments received on this aspect of the guidelines largely amounted to arguments that other means of classifying sex offenders would be better policy, such as reliance on risk assessments that take account of a broader range of factors than those authorized in the SORNA tier definitions. As described and advocated in these comments, such alternative systems would involve less consistency and predictability in sex offender registration and notification requirements, and would make available less information (or no information) concerning many sex offenders to the authorities or the public. The comments do not establish that these systems represent a sounder balancing of interests than the standards enacted in SORNA. In any event, the adoption of such alternative classification systems cannot be regarded as substantial implementation of SORNA insofar as they entail registration and notification requirements that fall below the SORNA minimum requirements—see the discussion above in connection with Part II.E of the guidelines—and hence cannot be authorized by the guidelines.

Some comments received from Indian tribes or tribal organizations objected to the uniform treatment of tribal sex offense convictions as supporting only "tier I" classification for SORNA purposes. They noted that this results from the federal law limitation of tribal court jurisdiction to misdemeanor penalties, though the underlying sex offense may be serious and would result in felony penalties if prosecuted in a state jurisdiction or the federal jurisdiction. This feature of the guidelines cannot be changed because it is statutory. SORNA § 111(2)-(4) classifies sex offenders as tier II or tier III only on the basis of offenses punishable by imprisonment for more than one year. However, as with other features of SORNA, the requirements associated with the tier I classification constitute only minimum standards. Tribal jurisdictions and other jurisdictions are free to prescribe more extensive registration and notification requirements for sex offenders convicted of tribal offenses, taking into account the substantive nature of the offenses or other factors, notwithstanding the misdemeanor status of the offenses in terms of the maximum permitted penalty. The final guidelines make this point more explicitly.

Responding to other comments received, changes have also been made in Part V to: (i) clarify further that the elements of the offense of conviction may be relied on in making tier classifications, except with respect to victim age; (ii) clarify the operation of tier enhancements based on recidivism, where the earlier conviction supporting a higher tier classification occurred prior to the enactment of SORNA or its implementation in a particular jurisdiction; and (iii) emphasize that the tier classification criteria do not constitute independent requirements to register offenders for whom SORNA does not otherwise require registration.

VI.   Required Registration Information

Registration Information Requirements Added by the Guidelines

Some commenters objected globally to the guidelines' requirement that the sex offender registries obtain certain types of information that are not expressly required by SORNA §114, such as e-mail addresses and comparable Internet identifiers, telephone numbers, temporary lodging information, travel document information, professional license information, and date of birth information. The guidelines have not been changed on this point. Many of these comments projected that sex offenders would be exposed to harassment or other adverse consequences because of the public disclosure of such information, reflecting an incorrect assumption that SORNA or the guidelines would require that all such information be posted on the public sex offender websites. The actual website posting requirements under the guidelines are more limited, and the final guidelines have been revised to make this point with greater clarity, as discussed in connection with Part VII of the guidelines below. All of the additional items are within the scope of the Attorney General's express statutory authority to require additional registration information. *See* SORNA § 114(a)(7), (b)(8). All are justified as means of furthering SORNA's public safety objectives, as the guidelines explain in their discussion of the additional required information.

Tribal Concerns

Many of the comments received from Indian tribes or tribal organizations objected to a specification in the proposed guidelines that the names and aliases that sex offenders are required to register include "traditional names given by family or clan pursuant to ethnic or tribal tradition." The purpose of this provision was to ensure that the registration information would include the names by which sex offenders are commonly known in their communities. It was not intended to require registration or disclosure of secret names of religious or ceremonial significance, and such names are not needed to further the purposes of sex offender registration and notification. The final guidelines have accordingly modified the description of this requirement so as to limit it to ethnic or tribal names by which the sex offender is commonly known.

Some of the tribal commenters also expressed concern about the requirements relating to DNA information from sex offenders, describing situations in which tribal communities had been misled about the uses that would be made of DNA samples they provided. However, SORNA's requirement on this point, as the guidelines explain, is only that jurisdictions ensure that DNA samples are collected from sex offenders for purposes of analysis and inclusion in the Combined DNA Index System (CODIS). The normal rules and procedures for DNA information in CODIS are tailored to its use for law enforcement identification purposes, such as matching a perpetrator's DNA collected from crime scene evidence to DNA taken from an offender. These rules and procedures are adequately designed to ensure that the analysis of collected DNA samples and entry of the resulting DNA profiles into CODIS cannot be used for the improper purposes that concern the commenters, such as ascertaining the incidence of genetic traits or disorders in communities or population groups from which the DNA samples are derived.

Requests for Clarification

Some commenters requested additional guidance or clarification regarding particular types of required registration information, such as the information concerning travel and immigration documents, and the statutory requirement to include information concerning addresses at which the sex offender "will" be an employee. The final guidelines provide further explanation or clarification on these points.

VII. Disclosure and Sharing of Information

Some of the comments reflected misapprehensions that the guidelines would require public disclosure of a broader range of sex offender information than is actually the case. The guidelines identify a limited number of informational items concerning sex offenders that must be included on the public sex offender websites, essentially covering name information, address or location information, vehicle information, physical description, sex offenses for which convicted, and a current photograph. Other types of registration information are within the scope of either mandatory or discretionary exemptions from required public disclosure. The relevant discussion in the final guidelines has been revised for greater clarity on this point.

Some commenters objected specifically to the required public disclosure of the addresses of employers of registered sex offenders, arguing that this information should be exempted from website posting, either on a discretionary or mandatory basis. SORNA itself requires that the registration information for sex offenders include employer name and address, but provides a discretionary exemption from public website posting for employer name only (not employer address). *Compare* SORNA § 114(a)(4), *with* SORNA § 118(c)(2). The SORNA provisions on this point reflect an accommodation of competing interests. On the one hand, requiring website posting of employer name could tar an employer based on the association with the sex offender and deter employers from hiring sex offenders. On the other hand, disclosing no employment-related information or only limited employment-related information could leave the public unaware concerning sex offenders' presence in places where they actually spend much of their time (e.g., 40 hours a week for a sex offender with a full-time job). SORNA accommodates these interests by requiring that the public websites include employer address information, but leaving it in the discretion of jurisdictions whether they will include employer name information as well. The comments received provide no adequate basis for the guidelines to second-guess this legislative judgment concerning the proper accommodation of these interests, even assuming that there would be legal authority to do so.

VIII. Where Registration Is Required

The portion of the guidelines relating to the jurisdictions in which registration is required has been edited to a limited extent for clarity on some points but has not been substantially changed. Some commenters misunderstood SORNA and the guidelines as requiring continued registration with the original jurisdiction of conviction even if the sex offender has no present residence, employment, or school attendance relationship with that jurisdiction. Some took "jurisdiction" as including political subdivisions of states, and consequently believed that SORNA prescribes requirements as to the particular locations within states in which sex offenders must be required to register—e.g., in which particular county or counties. SORNA itself and the proposed guidelines do not provide any support for these misconceptions, and additional language has been included in the final guidelines to guard against continued misunderstandings of this type.

IX. Initial Registration

The discussion in this Part has been expanded in the final guidelines to explain the statutory requirement in section 117(a) of SORNA that initial registration of incarcerated sex offenders is to be carried out "shortly before release."

Some commenters expressed concern about initial registration in relation to sex offenders whose predicate sex offense convictions predate the enactment of SORNA or its implementation in a particular jurisdiction. The guidelines require registration of such sex offenders in conformity with SORNA if they remain in the system as prisoners, supervisees, or registrants, or if they later reenter the system because of a subsequent criminal conviction. The commenters' concerns focused heavily on the fourth category—sex offenders who were fully out of the system at the time of SORNA implementation, but later reenter it based on conviction for some other crime. Concerns were expressed that registration of offenders in this category would require jurisdictions to examine the criminal histories of all new criminal convicts indefinitely to ascertain whether they have a sex offense conviction somewhere in the past that would require registration under the SORNA standards. A particular concern was that in cases in which the sex offense conviction occurred long ago, information about it might not be disclosed through an ordinary criminal history check, potentially necessitating extraordinary records search efforts to determine whether the offender must register. Concerns also were expressed about the adequacy of ordinary criminal history information to determine the extent of registration requirements under SORNA, including whether the sex offender's registration period has expired or still has time left to run. For example, whether the victim of a sexual contact offense was an adult or a minor may make the difference between the offender's classification as tier I or tier II under the SORNA standards, with consequent differences in the required registration period (15 years for tier I versus 25 years for tier II). But the criminal history information available in a case in which the sex offense conviction predated a jurisdiction's implementation of SORNA might show simply conviction of a sexual contact offense with no indication as to victim age.

The final guidelines address the foregoing concerns by clarifying that jurisdictions may rely on their normal methods and standards for obtaining and reviewing criminal history information, and on the information available in the records obtained by such means, in ascertaining SORNA registration requirements for sex offenders in the "retroactive" classes.

Some of the comments received from Indian tribes or tribal organizations proposed that the Federal Bureau of Prisons should be responsible for initial registration of federal sex offenders who will be released to tribal areas. However, there is a more limited statutory release procedure for federal sex offenders under 18 U.S.C. 4042(c), which requires the Federal Bureau of Prisons or federal probation offices to notify sex offenders of their registration requirements under SORNA around the time of their release or sentencing. That provision further requires the Bureau of Prisons and the federal probation offices to notify state and local law enforcement and registration agencies in the destination jurisdictions, which include tribal jurisdictions for sex offenders released to tribal areas. The failure of such a sex offender to appear in the destination jurisdiction and register as required would be reportable to federal authorities as provided in Part XIII of the guidelines, and would generally result in investigation of the matter by federal supervision or law enforcement authorities. In the normal situation in which the released federal sex offender does appear in the destination jurisdiction as required, that jurisdiction would register the sex offender as it does sex offenders entering from other jurisdictions.

X.   Keeping the Registration Current

Some commenters expressed concern about requiring sex offenders to report changes of certain types of registration information through in-person appearances. For example, SORNA §113(c) requires that changes of employment be reported through in-person appearances within three business days. Consider the effect, for example, in relation to a sex offender who obtains work—e.g., construction work or other manual labor—by showing up each morning at a site that contractors visit to recruit day labor. If the sex offender's employer varied day to day, the requirement to report changes in employment through in-person appearances might effectively require the sex offender to make an in-person appearance to report his recent employment history every few days, with attendant burdens on the jurisdiction and the offender.

In relation to required registration information, the proposed guidelines recognized that sex offenders may reside somewhere without having definite residence addresses, and similarly that sex offenders may be employed without fixed or settled employment. For such cases, Part VI of the guidelines affords necessary flexibility by providing that jurisdictions are to obtain information concerning such transient residence or employment with whatever definiteness is possible under the circumstances. The final guidelines incorporate comparable provisions in Part X so as to afford jurisdictions flexibility in dealing with the reporting of changes in residence or employment by sex offenders whose residence or employment is transient in character.

Comments were also received concerning a potential gap in the reporting requirements for sex offenders who terminate residence, employment, or school attendance in a jurisdiction but do not have any definite expectation about residing, working, or attending school elsewhere. For example, consider the case of a transient sex offender who is moving out of a state in which he has been living, but cannot say in which state or other jurisdiction he will reside next. The proposed guidelines did not address the reporting requirements in such situations with adequate clarity. The final guidelines provide that the requirement for sex offenders to keep the registration current includes requiring them to report consistently the termination of residence, employment, or school attendance to the appropriate jurisdiction in which they have been registered, regardless of whether any new place of residence, employment, or school attendance can be identified.

Responding to comments and questions received, a final paragraph also has been added to Part X in the final guidelines to clarify further that the SORNA requirement that registrants report changes in registration information through in-person appearances pertains only to changes in name and to changes in residence, employment, or school attendance between or within jurisdictions. The manner in which sex offenders are to report other changes in registration information is a matter within jurisdictions' discretion.

XI. Verification/Appearance Requirements

The discussion of SORNA's requirement of periodic in-person appearances by registrants to verify and update registration information has not been substantially modified in the final guidelines because it did not draw extensive comments, and no comments received provided any persuasive reasons to change the discussion of this requirement. However, responding to comments about situations in which a registrant dies, a paragraph has been added to Part XI in the final guidelines to provide advice to jurisdictions about the updating of registration information and public website postings in such situations.

XII. Duration of Registration

As discussed in earlier portions of the summary, the explanation concerning the required duration of registration is revised in the final guidelines. The changes clarify further (i) the discretionary nature of tolling during subsequent periods in which the sex offender is in custody, and (ii) the discretion of jurisdictions to adopt registration periods that are longer than the required SORNA minimum.

XIII. Enforcement of Registration Requirements

The discussion of enforcement of registration requirements in the proposed guidelines has not been modified in the final guidelines because it did not draw extensive comment and the comments received did not provide any persuasive reasons to change this part.

Appendix B.   Title Reference to SORNA sections.

§102. Declaration of purpose

§111. Relevant definitions, including Amie Zyla expansion of sex offender definition and expanded inclusion of child predators.

§112. Registry requirements for jurisdictions.

§113. Registry requirements for sex offenders.

§114. Information required in registration.

§115. Duration of registration requirement.

§116. Periodic in person verification.

§117. Duty to notify sex offenders of registration requirements and to register.

§118. Public access to sex offender information through the internet.

§119. National Sex Offender Registry.

§120. Dru Sjodin National Sex Offender Public Website.

§121. Megan Nicole Kanka and Alexandra Nicole Zapp Community Notification Program

§122. Actions to be taken when sex offender fails to comply.

§123. Development and availability of registry management and website software.

§124. Period for implementation by jurisdictions.

§125. Failure of jurisdiction to comply.

§126. Sex Offender Management Assistance (SOMA) Program.

§127. Election by Indian tribes.

§128. Registration of sex offenders entering the United States.

§129. Repeal of predecessor sex offender program.

§141. Amendments to title 18, United States Code, relating to sex offender requirements.

§142. Federal assistance with respect to violations of registration requirements.

§144. Federal assistance in identification and location of sex offenders relocated as a result of a major disaster.

§146. Office of Sex Offender Sentencing, Monitoring, Apprehending, Registering and Tracking.

Appendix C.   Title Reference to Federal Statutes

18 U.S.C. 1162.	State jurisdiction over offenses committed by or against Indians in the Indian Country.
18 U.S.C. 1591.	Sex trafficking of children or by force, fraud or coercion.
18 U.S.C. 2241.	Aggravated sexual abuse.
18 U.S.C. 2242.	Sexual abuse.
18 U.S.C. 2244.	Abusive sexual contact.
18 U.S.C. 2246.	Definitions for chapter; (sexual abuse chapter).
18 U.S.C. 2250.	Failure to register.
18 U.S.C. 2422(b).	Coercion and enticement.
18 U.S.C. 2423(a).	Transportation of minors with intent to engage in criminal sexual activity.
18 U.S.C. 3521.	Witness relocation and protection.
18 U.S.C. 3563(a)(8).	Conditions of probation; for a person required to register under the Sex Offender Registration and Notification Act.
18 U.S.C. 3583(d).	Conditions of supervised release.
18 U.S.C. 4042(c).	Duties of Bureau of Prisons; notice of sex offender release.
42 U.S.C. 3750.	Name of program; Edward Byrne Memorial Justice Assistance Grant Program.
42 U.S.C. 5119(a).	Reporting child abuse crime information

INDEX